APACHE LEGENDS

Songs of the Wind Dancer

Lou Cuevas

Library of Congress Cataloging-in-Publication Data

Cuevas, Lou, 1946-
Apache Legends: Songs of the Wind Dancer
    p.   cm.
1. Apache Indians--Legends. I. Title
E99.A6C84 1991
3098.2'089972--dc20   91-3 1366
                                                                    CIP

ISBN 13: 978-087961-219-1
ISBN 10: 087961-219-3

Cover painting and illustrations by Fred Cleveland

Seventh printing 2014

Naturegraph Publishers has been publishing books on
natural history, Native Americans, and outdoor subjects
since 1946. Free catalog available

Naturegraph Publishers, Inc.
PO Box 1047 ● 3543 Indian Creek Rd.
Happy Camp, CA 96039
(530) 493-5353
www.naturegraph.com

Books for a better world

*This book is dedicated to my grandfather,
Jhuna Ta-Ta Che, who, with his stories,
inspired pride in my people, my land,
and my heritage.
His spirit is the essence of my song.*

CONTENTS

Introduction

When I was a boy, my grandfather took me for a walk along the banks of a river. It was after sunset, during the early spring, and a new moon was rising slowly, casting a glimmering reflection on the slow moving waters. The landscape was eerie and foreboding with tall dogwood reeds, fuzzy cattails, and water spears standing like advance guards. As we walked, Grandfather spoke to me about the many wonders bequeathed to us by our Apache forebears.

One such gift, he said, was taught to him by his grandfather. It was called the song of the Wind Dancer. This song, he explained, was one of many and it would beseech the Water Spirit to honor a pledge made centuries before. In that far ancient time, a water spirit was found frozen in ice by an Apache warrior called Wind Dancer. The spirit promised to share his magic with the warrior, if he was released. Building a fire, Wind Dancer soon freed the water spirit. In gratitude, the spirit taught the warrior many magical songs which have since been handed down to his descendants.

Now, as we walked along the river bank, my grandfather, himself an Apache medicine man, said he would teach me one such song. Anxious to possess the power of our ancestors, I eagerly watched and listened in silence as Grandfather selected a break in the reed-covered banks. Spying, and then snatching a large plump bullfrog from its concealment, Grandfather knelt at the river's edge. Holding the frog in his upwardly, outstretched hands, he began to sing. His chant was rich and strong. It began slowly, rising and falling in pitch and volume.

Awaken all you night spirits! Awaken and hear my song. I call upon the Water Spirit to hear my prayer, for I am Jhuna Ta-Ta Che, medicine chief of the Sand People, son of a desert mother and blood descendant of the Wind Dancer who was promised a share from the abundance of the waters. Hear me, Great One! My family is in need of food. Grant me the miracle of life and allow us the presence of your children. In return mine will honor you always.

As Grandfather ended his song, I observed him gently stroking the small prickly spine of the bullfrog. At the same time, he brought it close to his face, saying, "Go my friend, take my prayer to your father. Let him know of my plea and return quickly with his answer."

Then, he released the squirming amphibian into the dark waters allowing the tiny waves to wash his hands. As he arose, he stepped away, nudging me back. While we waited, he chanted quietly, and I imagined what a water spirit might look like. I had just completed a picture in my mind, when an amazing phenomenon occurred. Approaching my grandfather's feet were dozens upon dozens of leaping, croaking bullfrogs coming out from the river. As Grandfather knelt to select a few for our table, I stood in disbelief and utter astonishment. I was completely awed by his magic and wondered for a long moment if he might be a God.

For years afterwards, I was convinced Grandfather was an extraordinary being. No other adult in my life had so great an influence over my imagination. His knowledge was extensive. I frequently spent many hours with him during which he taught me Apache mythology and ancestral beliefs--specifically about the many creatures which the Apache considered an integral part of their world. These stories intrigued me the most. Each time I inquired about an animal, he detailed its origins and how it had evolved from a legendary people whom he often referred to as the "ancient ones."

The "ancient ones," which my Grandfather spoke of, were understood in Apache tradition to be the spirit race who were responsible for originating the spiritual and cultural values of my people. This race is now believed to be the spiritual powers that exist in and animate the natural world, and may be contacted through prayer.

Archaeologists say that the Apache are the descendants of Athabascan-speaking peoples who migrated through the Bering Strait more than 2,000 years ago. Entering the North American continent, they journeyed southward along the

Rocky Mountains. Later, dividing into three distinct groups, one group migrated back into Canada and Alaska, the second group moved west along the northern Pacific coast, while the third group entered the Southwest becoming the six Apache tribes and their cousins, the Navajo. Although now associated with territory in Arizona and New Mexico, the Apache homeland once extended north into Colorado and Kansas and south into Mexico.

Among the tribes of New Mexico was that of my grandfather's parents, who had blood ties in Arizona. Family members confirm that these people were a remnant clan, ostensively from the White Mountain region. Unfortunately, in the 1870s, the Apache encountered the United States Army and the equally destructive United States Politician. Their combined efforts sought to obliterate the Apache. One method was documentation. If Apache members resisted, they were relocated to such remote locales that future generations would find tracing their ancestry difficult, if not impossible. Another method was barbaric. Taking plague-infested blankets, U.S. agencies "freely" distributed them among the tribes with disastrous results to the Apache.

The conflict continues. New factors serve to erode the Apache way of life. Where shortsighted government officials failed, modern materialism and religious fundamentalism are succeeding. They do so by ingesting the very seed of the Indian, namely his children. At present, the Apache, like other Indian nations, is virtually acculturated. Yet, final assimilation will overtake them only if future generations no longer recall their traditional ancestry, rites, and beliefs. Only when this legacy is consumed by Apache ambivalence will the people become obsolete. Thus the need for this and other similar books.

In completing this manuscript, I honor a promise to my grandparents. Grandmother, upon Grandfather's death, urged me to become a storyteller and to recite these legends (chanted as songs) which she and Grandfather learned as children but have waited seventy years before being written down. She reminded me that storytellers are an honored people purposely selected by the spirit of living things to chant atop special mountains, near rivers, waterfalls, and open campfires. She explained that the spirit song, which varies from tribe to tribe, is like a prayer, and the more reverent the location, the more the spirits will aid in the chant.

The legends told here, which explained nature, its manifestations, and human behavior, were taught to Indian children so that they might learn to respect the power of life. I remind the reader that these stories of the animal spirits are sacred to the Apache and should not be ridiculed.

In trying to preserve these stories, I beg the reader to understand that changing an oral chant into the written word does cause some distortion. But I recite with pride as best I can remember them. For you the reader, I have endeavored to preserve an ancient spirit people who are forever part of my blood heritage. I suppose that despite my diligence, I have left some stories frozen in time. For this, I apologize.

Lou Cuevas

(NOTE: One day, in a college science class, I inadvertently discovered the secret of my grandfather's magic. It seems that female frogs, when held in one's palm and stroked, will secrete pheromones which when applied to flowing waters will invariably attract males. Grandfather possessed this knowledge before colleges became mandatory!)

Legend of the Dream Woman

(Peyote)

Many legends reflect important tribal beliefs which become practiced outwardly in tribal rituals. One such ritual honors the story of a warrior called Fire Hawk and his trials with a powerful water spirit called the Dream Woman. These two mysterious figures, once common to only one tribe, are now part of the heritage of several others. Indeed, because of different tribal interpretations, this story often varies. However, the privilege of retelling it belongs to all.

The origin of the Dream Woman was first told by a storyteller who spoke of ancestors known as Dream People (Ndee Nabiyeeti). They inhabited a section of the Southwest known to nomadic tribes as the Ribs of the Earth. There, under the protective sphere of the Spirit Mountain (Dzit Diyini), they lived for a time in dangerous proximity to several marauding tribes.

Although the ancient Ndee were a proud people with many traditions, two characteristics typify them more than others. The first was their passionate belief that courage was the ultimate shield against any enemy. Any Ndee warrior in his prime would rather endure hours of brutal torture than risk showing the slightest trace of fear. Their second trademark was a strong belief in the power of wisdom. The tribespeople believed that anyone seeking wisdom should live by the maxim: "If one is old enough to seek good advice, one should be wise enough to follow it." This rule became the law for the Ndee. Why this fervent dedication? The answer lies in the legend of the Dream Woman.

11

The Ndee had wandered for many years as they migrated southward from the northern woodlands into the expansive deserts and prairies of the Southwest. Having spent the better part of five years in search of a new place to settle, they found a sheltered valley at the foot of a high, forested mountain. Within the shadow of this towering sentinel's encircling arms, they established their camp.

When the Ndee arrived, they numbered some fifteen hundred people. Though they were a peaceful and trusting tribe, they had experienced their share of brutal conflicts, and they were vigilant against reprisals. This wary attitude led to the creation of an exemplary type of warrior. In courage, skill, and fighting ability, the Ndee warrior had few equals.

While the men trained and earned their warrior rank, the women performed many useful and specific tasks. Among them was the daily chore of gathering firewood. In time, as they gained a working knowledge of the landscape, the women learned that the best area for gathering firewood was in the more difficult recesses of the nearby mountain.

One day, when the women went foraging in the upper mountain, they chanced upon a hidden cove wherein they discovered a wondrous blue waterfall. They watched in awe as the upper icy waters crashed to the smooth rocks below, creating a hazy mist. The women, having worked all day, went to drink from the water when, without warning, the earth rumbled and quaked, causing them to scatter away in panic. Later, discovering that one of the women had not returned, they informed their chief.

The chief of the Ndee was named Red Shadow. For thirty years he had led his people with a firm and just hand. Everyone admired his courage, and the council respected his wisdom. Red Shadow was an old man of sixty years, but his graying hair did not lessen his handsome features. These features had attracted and won the heart of his wife, Gentle Wind, whose love had remained strong for her husband throughout the thirty years of his leadership. It was Gentle Wind who had often soothed her husband's troubled brow. It was she who had softened his moments of rage and awakened his compassion and understanding. But most important, Gentle Wind had borne her husband a strong, healthy son, who became his greatest joy.

Red Shadow and Gentle Wind beamed with pride as their son was accepted into the tribe. They stood proud when they first heard his name, Fire Hawk, stated aloud by the medicine man. Throughout their lives, when their son took his first steps, snared his first rabbit, or returned triumphant from his first hunt, his parents basked in the glory of his achievements. Now in their twilight years, Red Shadow and Gentle Wind saw Fire Hawk attain the status of manhood.

Fire Hawk was a tall, strong, bronze-skinned warrior. Though he stood slightly taller than his father, his respect for his parents never dimmed. The care of his mother and father came first, followed by his duty to perfect the skills of the hunter and warrior. In addition, Fire Hawk received wise counsel from his mentor, Yellow Wolf, the medicine man.

The noonday sun was peering through a thinly overcast sky, the day the frightened Ndee women came running down from the mountain. With all of the women trying to speak at the same time, their voices resembled the shrill sounds of migratory birds assembling in the marshes. Their excited cries attracted everyone in the camp to come and hear what they were saying. Soon, word of the commotion reached the chief.

With his wife beside him, Red Shadow stood outside his tepee and watched curiously as a growing crowd of Ndee approached his tent. Upon reaching him, the women sobbed out their story, recounting what they had experienced at the waterfall and how they later discovered that one of their number had not returned. "She must have been killed," they finished. "Who was?" asked the chief."Dream Woman," they replied. Completing their account, the women returned to their tepees.

Later, a gathering of the council to discuss the disappearance of Dream Woman ended with a proposal. The council asked Red Shadow if he could send an escort to protect the women the next time they gathered wood. Red Shadow agreed and decided to send his son. Fire Hawk accepted the challenge and chose ten braves to accompany him.

The following day, after an hour of climbing, the group reached the cove and the hidden waterfall. While the women gathered their firewood, the warriors entered the cove and attempted to find the missing body of Dream Woman. Suddenly the ground began to shake violently and the water in the falls turned bright red. At the same time, the trees surrounding the waterfall glowed as though they were on fire!

The violent shaking of the earth tumbled all the warriors near the falls. Those who could, ran, fell, or crawled away from the epicenter. Although he had been forced to the ground, Fire Hawk managed to rise and hold a half kneeling position from where he stared into the beautiful red waterfall. Fire Hawk marveled at the flaming trees, which reflected their luminous shapes in his dark eyes. Then with his hands extended in front of him, he moved toward the ring of stones near the base of the falls where he reached out and curiously touched the ruby colored water.

"Have you no fear!" questioned a shrill female voice.

"If this was meant to frighten me," replied Fire Hawk, searching for the source of the voice, "you do not know me!"

"Tell me about yourself!" demanded the voice.

"I am Fire Hawk, son of Red Shadow, chief of the Ndee! It is our camp at the foot of this mountain. I am not afraid! It is not my nature."

"Would you prove this courage, foolish one," challenged the voice. "Would you risk all that you hold dear on its value?"

"Show yourself to me," shouted Fire Hawk, still searching for the source of the voice. "How do I know you are real and not merely a dream? Come, show me what power holds my friends, frightens our women, and dares to challenge me!"

Abruptly, the cascading waters stopped falling and began to flow upward, forming the misty figure of a woman. The fiery trees grew brighter, and Fire Hawk felt their intense heat against his skin. The ground stopped shaking while the hissing waters steamed, forming a ring above the figure's shoulders where the head should be. Inside the ring, Fire Hawk saw the distorted, watery face of an old woman appear. "Dream Woman," he exclaimed, recognizing the image.

The steamy waters flowing down the sides of Dream Woman's face looked like braids of silver hair. Rising slowly from the ground, Fire Hawk stood, clutching a war club in one hand and a knife in the other. Instinctively, he knew that they would be of little use against such power. Still, they reassured him, and he maintained a tight grip on them. Looking up at the towering figure, he saw that her face had cleared. Now he was certain it was the face of the missing woman.

"Well, young brave," asked the watery voice, "have you satisfied your curiosity? Are you still willing to gamble all on your courage."

"You are Dream Woman," he shouted. "You are the one we have come to find. They said you were dead. How is it you are part of this magic?"

"I have always been here," she explained. "My spirit walked among you for a time, but I have always been here in these waters, waiting for you."

"What is it you wish of me?" he asked, expecting to be killed.

"I wish to test you. In doing so, I test your people. Therefore, I will send into your camp a darkness, one that is man's greatest foe and can destroy him. You must battle against it, lest it destroy your people. Further, my brothers will meet you in combat. If you fail against them, the fate of your people will be sealed. Do you accept?"

"I accept your challenge," shouted Fire Hawk. "But how will I know if I have won?" he asked as she began to fade. "How will I know if I have saved my people? What must I learn from the darkness?"

"You will know if you have failed," Dream Woman responded, "because your failure will empty your heart, and the world will feel like the wind. If you succeed, you will know it and your heart will give your success a name. Now go! See if your courage matches your boast!"

When Fire Hawk returned from the mountain, many in the tribe were anxious to hear of his incredible encounter with the thunderous waterfall. The curious pressed about him tightly and excitedly questioned him. Sensing he needed help, his companions cleared a path for him until at last he stood before the tepee of his parents. The tribe, his parents, the elders, and Yellow Wolf were there waiting to hear his experience.

"What did the water spirit ask of you," questioned Red Shadow.

After he explained the connection between the falls, the water spirit, and Dream Woman, Fire Hawk had difficulty remembering more. "She challenged me to..." Then in a flash, his mind went blank. There were no further details in his mind. Only vague images. For long painful moments, he struggled to recall the details, but he could not remember them. Ashamed and confused, he asked to be left alone.

"What troubles Fire Hawk," the council wanted to know.

"The water spirit has clouded his memory," suggested the medicine man. "He now battles her for control of his thoughts."

"Red Shadow, help our son!" Gentle Wind requested. "He is still young."

"But he wears the mantle of a man," countered Red Shadow proudly. "The water spirit has emptied his thoughts, not his heart. His inner power, that which we call the manitou, must now awaken."

With Fire Hawk walking away from the camp, and Yellow Wolf following, the chief asked his people to return home. The warriors who had accompanied Fire Hawk to the mountain were questioned by the dispersing crowd. For several days, Fire Hawk wandered, alone and confused, trying to piece together his thoughts. Always close behind the bewildered brave was his medicine friend, Yellow Wolf. For now, all he could do was wait until the troubled warrior asked for advice. Such was the way of his people.

Finally, after a week of trying to unravel the mystery by himself, Fire Hawk came to the medicine man's lodge. Upon entering, he sat across from the shaman. Fire Hawk then told the old one of his inability to overcome the water spirit's power and asked if there was some way to fight her magic. Yellow Wolf advised the troubled warrior to journey into the desert, far beyond the sight of the mountain, then, when he was too tired to continue, he should make camp exactly where he stopped. The medicine man advised Fire Hawk to take a pouch of spring water but no food. Yellow Wolf warned him to eat only what he found beneath his bedding blanket.

With a pouch of water and no food, Fire Hawk walked into the desert until he no longer saw the mountain. After many days of aimless wandering, he fell, exhausted. Recalling Yellow Wolf's advice, Fire Hawk put his blanket down and marked off its width and length. Then he moved the blanket, scratched at the scrubby earth, pulled up a plant, and ate the soft root. At once he fell asleep and slept for days, dreaming of painted warriors waiting for him on a snowy mountain.

Upon awakening, Fire Hawk felt refreshed. Instantly, he remembered the challenge of the water spirit. He also became aware of the biting wind and cold, and noticed that the ground as far as he could see was covered with snow. "Snow? In the middle of summer? How could that be," he wondered. Rising, he wrapped himself in his blanket and began the long trip back to the camp of his people. Despite frigid conditions and his dwindling strength, he was able to make his way home. When he arrived, he was shocked by what he saw.

The specter of death lay heavy on the faces of Red Shadow and his wife as they stared at their returning son. The entire camp of the Ndee was in ruins. Hundreds of tepees were burned and piles of dead bodies lay scattered throughout the camp. Among the tents still standing was his father's. Fire Hawk entered and then sat down, dazed by the gruesome sight. As he listened in silence, the following facts were revealed to him:

"You have been gone six months, my son," said his father sadly. "Our people have been at war with many tribes. A dozen braves have spent weeks looking for you. We had given you up when the dark snow came. Now a stench of death encircles our camp, killing our people. We realize that you have been unaware of these events, but perhaps now you have discovered what power holds the land and threatens us with destruction."

"That is what I was challenged to overcome, my father," replied Fire Hawk. "The Dream Woman has set us against the dark spirits."

"But how can you defeat them, my son," questioned his mother.

"The answer was given to Fire Hawk in a dream," explained Yellow Wolf confidently. "That was the reason he could not remember before. Now he does."

Without hesitation, Fire Hawk arose, promising he would not return until the enemies of his people had been defeated. After changing into his battle clothes and adding special paint to his features, he took up the weapons of war. Then he left, climbing to the snowy summit of the Spirit Mountain. When he arrived, he called out to the mountain spirits to come and fight him to the death. Walking deeper into its dark forest, he repeated the challenge. Suddenly, Fire Hawk saw a group of four Indian warriors approaching him.

"They are all chiefs," Fire Hawk concluded as he observed the warriors more closely. The strangers wore beautifully decorated war bonnets. Their shields had the designs of the eagle, the bear, the wolf, and the snake engraved on them. Their headpieces were shaped like the animals they represented. Their somber faces were painted with colorful patterns. Two of the warriors had spears in addition to knives and heavy war clubs. The other two held only knives and war clubs. Because of their painted features, Fire Hawk could not make out their faces. The forest was quiet, yet the wind in the trees reminded Fire Hawk of Dream Woman's laughing, taunting voice.

Three of the chiefs stood back while the bear warrior stepped forward to meet Fire Hawk alone. Taking a firm grip on his war club, Fire Hawk gave a loud war cry and ran toward the spirit, who responded in like manner. Rushing toward one another in the snow was easier than it appeared, and seconds later, Fire Hawk realized his foe was no phantom. His opponent's spiked club tore at Fire Hawk's shield and their bodies collided with bruising force. As soon as the two struck together, the bear-warrior began savagely raining blows on Fire Hawk, who deflected them with his battered shield and struck back when he could. The two warriors fought fiercely and desperately until, at last, Fire Hawk gained an advantage and clubbed his foe, knocking him unconscious.

Examining the fallen warrior, Fire Hawk rested briefly before the second chief charged him with avenging fury. Resembling an eagle, he sped forward as if hurling from a great height. Fire Hawk quickly regripped his war club, and crouched in anticipation. The screaming chief crashed into Fire Hawk, who absorbed the impact. Then, like determined rams, the combatants hammered at one another until their war clubs met above them, shattering. When the agile chief reached for his knife, Fire Hawk seized him with a stranglehold.

After an intense struggle, Fire Hawk felt his enemy go limp. But no sooner had he released the eagle-warrior's body than he was pierced by a spear through the left shoulder. Grasping the long shaft, he gritted his teeth and pulled it out. As he knelt and raised his ragged shield, the third chief slammed him to the ground. Fire Hawk saw the wolf's face glaring behind his opponent's slashing blade, and he was barely able to check the glinting point. Then, with a superhuman burst of energy, Fire Hawk lifted up the wolf-faced chief and sent him careening backward into a large boulder, snapping his spine.

Fire Hawk was exhausted. He rose unsteadily and paused to examine his wounds, when the fourth chief unexpectedly struck his back with a heavy war club. Slumping forward, Fire Hawk fell but managed to turn to restrain his now knife-wielding enemy. Taking two deep wounds to the chest, Fire Hawk struggled to defend himself. The snowy earth below numbed his pain and slowed his bleeding but failed to rejuvenate him. With the snake chief above him, forcing his blood-stained knife closer and closer to Fire Hawk's neck, he considered singing his death chant.

The world spun wildly, and Fire Hawk felt fear and darkness tugging at his resolve. Then, the faces of his parents appeared in his mind, and again, he heard the mocking laughter of the Dream Woman. The memory of her laughter filled him with fiery anger. Forcing his torn hand to respond, he plunged his bloodied knife into the snake-warrior, who clamped on to Fire Hawk's neck and squeezed. Gasping for air, Fire Hawk slashed his opponent's throat, covering the white landscape with blood. The snake warrior drooped forward as Fire Hawk struggled out from underneath him and crawled to a nearby tree. There he turned to stare at the unmoving bodies. He felt alone. The icy air whipped at his aching, battered body. A dozen wounds screamed for attention, yet as the sunlight faded and the shadows of the forest crept in, he decided to sleep.

With the morning sun warming and soothing his mangled body, Fire Hawk awakened to the glaring light which shimmered off the snowy landscape. Gazing about, he noticed that the ground showed no trace of the night's events. As he examined the blanket he lay on, a glowing figure appeared several yards away. It was Dream Woman. "Can you feel the wind in your heart," she asked.

"I do not!" answered Fire Hawk.

"Can you feel the darkness?"

"I feel only the sun," he replied.

"What then is the greatest foe of man?" she asked again.

"Fear," he responded.

"Did you defeat it?" she persisted.

"No," he said thoughtfully. "It can only be controlled."

"Then give this strength a name, Fire Hawk," she ordered.

"Knowledge," he proclaimed. "With it man controls his destiny."

"Your abilities match your wisdom," she finished. "You have proven the Ndee warrior to be the epitome of strength, skill, and courage."

"And the mountain spirits?" he asked as she began to fade.

"They did not die, but they did leave you some gifts as token of your victory. Your people need never be afraid as long as they possess these gifts."

Descending from the Spirit Mountain, Fire Hawk learned that Red Shadow and his braves had defeated the marauding bands and all disease had disappeared from the camp. As Fire Hawk walked through the restored camp, the gathering people gasped at the sight of his wounds. Anxious to learn what had happened, they followed close behind him to hear how he had fared against the Dream Woman and her brothers.

However, aside from sharing the details of his experience with Dream Woman and her brothers, Fire Hawk kept silent about the special gifts he had received. It was not until weeks later, during a ceremony honoring the mountain spirits, that he revealed them. The gifts included the very land on which they lived and extended to the horizon, the Spirit Mountain, a magical root (which would allow them to see into the future), and the prophecies concerning the Iron Man and the Faceless One. "The Iron Man will come seeking wealth," he explained. "Yet when he has it, he will not see it.

He will be followed by the Faceless One, who will promise peace but will leave only the wind."

Such were the gifts of the mountain spirits, who receded in time as their prophecies came to pass. The early Spanish explorers are believed by many to be the fulfillment of the coming of the Iron Man. Although the conquistadors came seeking wealth, they never realized the vast treasures they had acquired and lost until centuries later. The Faceless One is said to have been the white man, who with his many treaties promised peace but left only the wind in the once proud homeland of the American Indian.

The Spirit Mountain can be found on the Fort Apache Reservation in Arizona, and it is still considered part of the "Ribs of the Earth," better known as the Rocky Mountains. As for the Ndee, or the Apache, at the turn of the century the young men of the tribe in their quest for manhood still participated in many sacred ceremonies, perfected the warrior's arts, and also experienced a visit from the Dream Woman (Peyote Woman) via the peyote root, which induced a dreamlike trance, allowing them to "see" the future. Hence the name of the Ndee, the "Dream People."

Legend of the Swift Wind

(The Roadrunner)

Many ages ago, when the land belonged to the ancient Ndee, later known as the Apache, the Swift Wind story came into being. Since then, some have forgotten the tale, some do not understand it. Even today, among many clans, there are few who know of it. During ancient times it was forbidden for anyone except the Ndee to possess spirit knowledge. Yet now, as the yellow flames of time dance before you, I will speak the legend as it was related to me by my grandfather. It is a story about a wondrous creature whom the ancient ones called the Swift Wind.

Late in the summer, at the time of the Golden Moon, during the year of the Mating Wolf, when the boys of the Ndee tribe came to maturity, a great feast was called for. It was a time of harvest, a time of thanks, and a time known to them as the Choosing. The tribal elders were grateful that the Giver of Life, also called the Great or Sky Spirit, had blessed them during the year. Further, they knew that if theirs was to be a remembered nation, the youth of the tribe would have to win favor in a ceremonial dance. From it, the Great Spirit would choose the destiny of the boys.

Since the choosing was made from among the elder sons of the tribe, to them were made available the ornaments made by the young women. The girls brought them beaded jewelry, decorative paints, silver and gold bells, brightly embroidered deer skins, string belts, colorful moccasin boots, and very impressive war bonnets, all of which went into costumes that would please the Sky Spirit. Then an enormous bonfire was made ready in the center of the camp, a large number of drums were formed into a circle and finally, when all was ready, an offering of food and drink which was to be shared by the entire tribe was brought and the celebration began.

Displayed in their colorful costumes, the young men were cheered as they paraded into the camp center. Soon after, the drums created a beat and the boys began to dance, fashioning a festive mood as they chanted and encircled the great bonfire. As the celebration went on, the tribe moved to the rhythmic sounds of the booming drums which spoke of the Great Spirit. Eventually, everyone began singing praises to their great protector for their gifts, their health, and their joy. Hour after hour, the lively feasting continued while the sun set and the moon rose.

The hidden valley of the Ndee shook with a tremendous echo which reached high up into the night sky. There, in the shadow of the earth, watching his people, stood the Great Spirit. As he listened to their voices, he became pleased and smiled. So moved was the Sky Father by the mention of his name in their many songs that he took from his medicine pouch magic sky crystals and gently sprinkled them on the chosen boys.

Down in the valley, the elders of the tribe were pleased with their young men and admired them for their songs, their spirit, and their bright array. As the chief looked on the dancers, he saw not the boys but future hunters, guardians, and warriors of the tribe. In these same youths, the elders saw their replacements. The eyes of the tribal women saw their sons, their brothers, and, for many, their future husbands. This filled them with great pride. The joy in their hearts brought tears of happiness. Then all at once, they saw the black sky open up and it began to rain. But it was a strange sort of rain; it did not feel wet.

The tribe was amazed. Still the drums continued to beat and the boys continued to chant and dance. Faster and faster they went. As their bodies were ducking and bowing, their arms made gestures as if they were in flight. The flames of the fire began to grow and grow, and then, unexpectedly, to the utter astonishment of everyone who looked on, the brightly painted bodies of the boys started changing.

There were several thousand pairs of eyes in the valley that night. Before these eyes, the bodies of the boys began to grow feathers. Out from beneath their painted skin grew white, gold, brown, and black feathers changing them from boys into golden eagles. The transformation continued, with the decorated faces of the boys turning into the beaked faces of birds. Their small feet changed into the powerful claws of the famed fliers. Finally, the change was completed when the arms of each boy became the powerful wings of the bird of prey.

The drummers of the tribe had stopped their beat when they saw what was happening, yet by some unseen power the drums continued to send out a magical sound. As the drums played, the flames grew higher and higher until all at once, they exploded in a huge column of flame which shot the eagles high up into the sky. While all this was going on, no one gave much notice to one boy who, although he had grown feathers, did not look like an eagle and still danced round the fire all by himself. He was a bird, but he did not resemble the others.

The elders of the tribe and the rest of the people were in awe as they saw their young men flying in the full-moon night. From the eagles came a high shrill cry of joy and the people down below were filled with great pride. However, the chief of the tribe and then, soon after, the rest of the people noticed that one boy, a lad named Quo-Qui, meaning Swift Wind, was not flying above the fire. Indeed, he still continued to dance around the flaming circle completely unaware of anything or anyone around him. Everyone was puzzled.

Unaware as he was of their questioning stares, Quo-Qui remained on the ground oblivious to the other boys flying above him in the night sky. Saddened by the sight, the parents of Quo-Qui could not believe what they had witnessed. The elders were disappointed and the women were confused. The chief decided to consult with the medicine man. With the fire dying out, the boys who had changed into eagles came floating down and, once on the ground, ran triumphantly into their proud parent's arms. There was much happiness in their hearts. Yet in the eyes of Quo-Qui's parents, there was only doubt. Something was very wrong.

From that eventful day onward, the Ndee began to gossip about Quo-Qui and his disgrace. It was not bad enough that the boy felt ashamed and alone; to make him feel worse, there were many in the tribe who began to call him Runt Bird. Some believed that he had been cursed and should be driven out. Others suggested that perhaps Quo-Qui was not yet a man and, therefore, could not turn into an eagle. Numerous voices argued that Quo-Qui was outcast by the Great Spirit and should not be allowed to participate in any future ceremonial dances.

Whatever the views of the tribe, only one man had the power to change the law and that was the tribal chief. He more than anyone had heard the talk of his people and knew that he had to decide what was to be done. After consulting with the medicine man and the tribal elders, the chief informed his people that it had been the decision of the Great Spirit to turn Quo-Qui into a bird. Because he had feathers like the others, his people would have to be patient and wait for the Sky Father to show them why he had chosen Quo-Qui to be what he was. Only time would tell, he told them. Yet deep within his heart, the chief, too, had grave doubts, but he said nothing lest it change the future.

During the days which followed, the parents of Quo-Qui sat down with the boy and asked him if there was anything in his heart which would cause the Great Spirit to be angry with him. His mother cried and asked if there was some secret disgrace of which he had not told them. Quo-Qui's heart was heavy knowing that his own parents doubted his courage and honor. Did they not know their son well enough to realize that there was nothing for which he was ashamed? Still, seeing their grief, he explained that he could not remember anything about that night except that he was touched by the Great Spirit. He was unable to explain why he could not fly. Thereafter, his parents were sorry they had ever doubted their son and asked his forgiveness. Quo-Qui understood their concern and set out to solve his problem. But first he needed to hunt and this he did. With a fine prize in hand, he went to visit the only man who might explain the puzzle to him.

Quo-Qui's father had felt the sorrow carried by his son and advised him to seek out an explanation from the tribal medicine man. It would be he who could tell Quo-Qui what purpose the Great Spirit had for him. Following his father's counsel, the boy, with his gift in hand, went to see the mysterious but very wise medicine chief. Placing his catch before the tepee, he asked permission to speak to the holy man. The wife of the medicine man took the boy's offering and prepared a meal. After the two had eaten, the woman left them alone to talk.

The medicine man built a small fire in the center of the tepee. As the fire grew to its limits and then died out, the strangely painted man sang to the spirits who then whispered into his ears what they had heard about Quo-Qui. At the end of his song, the medicine man looked at the troubled Quo-Qui and told him what the spirits in the fire had said.

"There are those who seek to be great," the old man declared, "but in doing so, they become small. I see in the ashes that you are small, but in time you will be great."

"How can I be great, Holy One?" Quo-Qui questioned in disbelief. "I cannot fly! I am not made to look like my brothers! I am troubled by my people's laughter and, except for my parents, I am alone. There is a great weight in my heart. I do not understand."

"The Great Spirit guides your fate," the old man told him. "But he cannot control you heart. You have courage. Let it serve you now! The ashes tell me that you have been chosen. Nothing can change that. Your destiny awaits the moon; do not fight it."

"I do not doubt my courage, Holy One," replied Quo-Qui confidently. "I await my destiny. All I ask now is, have I dishonored myself? This I must know so that I may cleanse my spirit."

"Your fate is now in the wooded hills north of our camp," the medicine man advised. "There, within the empty bellies of our brothers who cry out in the wind, lies your future. But do not seek it, for even now it approaches. You have not been dishonored, but will bring honor. If you are now alone, it is because on the day of trial you will be alone. Go my son. Allow your heart to remember that true courage is the greatest shield."

Days passed and the boy endured all the laughter which came to him. Quo-Qui's parents were proud of their son who still walked tall through the camp. Soon a new moon rose and the day of trial arrived.

Since the first celebration of the Choosing there had been other celebrations. Each was a ceremony to give thanks or to ask the Great Spirit for something. During the Eagle Dance in which the chosen were seen, the result was always the same. The other boys were magically changed into great eagles except for Quo-Qui. So discouraged did he become that he told the others that he would not join in any longer. No one argued otherwise. Quo-Qui's spirit was in deep despair, even on the day when the chief sent all of his hunters on a five-day hunt for game.

Left behind in the camp were the women, the children, and the aged who could not fend for themselves. The chosen boys of the Eagle were given the task of guarding the camp against intruders. All of them eagerly took their assigned positions throughout the camp. Yet when Quo-Qui asked the oldest boy where he should go to stand guard, he received only laughs and jeers and was told to go and hide with the women and children where his little feathers would not show his disgrace. Quo-Qui became very angry, but he said nothing as he turned and walked away. Behind him he could hear the others call him names. He felt completely alone.

So loud was the growing laughter that few heard the frightful howl of starvation coming down from the nearby woodlands. It was the terrible cry of a great timber wolf. Joining this awful whine came the added growls of many other wolves, all of which sounded terribly close. Down in the camp, the people recognized the cry of the silver wolf and knew it meant they were searching for food. They also remembered that, when wolves went on the prowl, nothing short of death would keep them from their prey. The camp people grew horrified as certain destruction came closer and ever closer.

Numbering fifty in all, the silver-gray forms with their black manes came charging out from the thicket. They looked lean and savage. Their blood-red eyes glittered in the noonday sun. The entire camp panicked and everyone scattered for the shelter of their tents. As fear gripped the people, the Eagle boys looked at the howling pack and saw their long, sharp teeth. For a moment, they were hypnotized by the fearful sight.

Throughout the Ndee camp, the screams of frightened women and the wail of little children created a great din. Hearing it, the Eagle boys quickly gathered themselves to prepare a plan of defense. It was obvious that they were all that stood between the wolves and their people. Although the boys did not lack courage, they lacked a plan of action.

"What shall we do?" asked one.

"We must go for help!" suggested a second.

"We will all be dead by the time it arrives!" shouted another.

"We were given the task of defending the camp!" said the bravest of the boys. "It is clear, we must die to save our people."

"Our brother, the wolf, does not understand who we are," announced the eldest of the group. "Therefore, we shall perform our sacred Eagle dance and change into our Eagle form, proving that we are the chosen of the Great Spirit. Then, they will be too frightened to do any harm!"

"Yes!" encouraged another. "When they see us fly above them, they will become fearful and run away! Let's hurry, because our campfire burns low!"

All the boys agreed and were too busy to notice that Quo-Qui had joined in the dance as well. The chanting began while the murderous wolves were moving steadily into the camp. Once inside, the wolves immediately stopped. There before them was a strange sight. Instead of running for their lives, the boys had chosen to dance. Despite their hunger, the wolves waited, suspecting a trap. Then, when nothing happened, the wolves again bounded forward toward the group. All at once, the boys changed into eagles and shot up into the sky above them.

However, instead of being impressed, the wolves only became annoyed that some of their prey had gotten away. They did not understand the dance and what was more important, they were not frightened by the magical transformation. Ironically, the boys had not realized that once in the air, the eagles could do little against the wolves except to cry out in their high shrill voices and distract them with their claws. The people in the camp saw that Quo-Qui, the boy they had ridiculed, alone remained to save them. The wolves readied themselves to devour the remaining people hiding in their tents. Then, they noticed a curious looking little bird still dancing on the ground in front of them.

Quo-Qui, who had changed into a bird, had not flown into the air. He remained and was still circling the fire with his dance. Round and round he went, creating such a distraction that the wolves decided he should be the first to die. Turning aside from the women and children, the great timber wolves regrouped and attacked the tiny bird in the center of the camp. That was what Quo-Qui was waiting for.

Peering through the flaps in their tents, the frightened people saw the silver hoard chasing the agile bird round and round the fire. With his little gray wings firmly outstretched, Quo-Qui kept himself just out of reach by shooting himself forward each time the wolves lunged at him. Finally, the tiny gray bird with the soft brown feathers turned away from the fire and headed away from the camp. The wolves, determined to catch him, went fast on his heels.

Each time the leader and the rest of the pack thought they were just within reach, they opened their powerful jaws and sprang for him. But each time the pack attacked, the little bird turned to the right or to the left and glided along on the air to land a few yards ahead of the surprised predators. The wolves became furious and increased their speed, sure that they could catch the tiny form. Little did they realize that the clever bird had by this time led them miles away from the camp.

At last, in one final desperate charge, the entire wolf pack formed into a wide semicircle and forced the streaking bird to smaller and smaller turns. Then, when they were sure that Quo-Qui could not turn, they all sprang forward in one massive leap, unaware that a sharp cliff lay ahead.

As before, when the pack sprang toward him, the speedy bird shot forward into the air. Unknowingly, the entire group vaulted into a great open canyon. Flying out into the immense gorge, the timber wolves fell quickly to their death on the rocks below, while Quo-Qui shooting farther, eventually glided slowly and softly to the canyon floor on the same tiny wings which had changed him into the fastest little bird in the Southwest.

The flying eagles, who had been following the chase, saw that their brother had been transformed into a magical bird that all men would forever after recognize as the Roadrunner.

Today, in memory of that event, the Apache look upon the story of the Roadrunner as a good example to pass on to their children. If one looks for greatness in size, one tends to overlook it.

CLEVELAND

Legend of the Vexing Visitor

(The Fly)

The lands of the Southwestern Indian are a great open domain. On it, dozens of desert tribes have maintained a peaceful, quiet, and solitary life. Among these desert dwellers are the Apache, who, for the most part, enjoy their solitude. The families are closely bonded and like their private affairs kept to themselves. Anything less is considered rude and impolite. This story centers on one woman who, because of her annoying habits, became the subject of a classic tale taught to young Apache children on the proprieties of life. It also illustrates how the Apache tried to explain the living creatures around them.

Kei-A-I, meaning visitor, was an old woman living now in her sixtieth year. She was small, very lean, bony, and ill-kept. Her rugged face, which appeared scarred, reddish brown, and wind-burned, matched her limp old clothes. To say that she was a walking, talking, bundle of rags would have been a kindness. She was a terrible sight and yet, deep within her, there beat the heart of an overly friendly spirit.

It was the custom among Apache women to be the first to rise from the comfort of their beds. Once up, the crisp air gave them reason for building a fire out of the previous night's coals in the center of the tepee. Then they dressed very warmly, grabbed a bucket, and braving the outside air, went down to the river's edge for water. After getting the water, the women would trudge back up to the tent to prepare the morning meal. Since this was a daily chore, it came as no surprise that the women would meet each other coming and going. However, because of the drudgery, the

33

distance, and the cold, there were few greetings beyond that of an occasional nod or wave.

There are few people in the world who enjoy chatting in the cold. And Apache women, although as durable as their menfolk, prefer a warm fire to an icy wind. To them, the sooner out of the unpleasantness, the better. How Kei-A-I could bear up to the chilly mountain wind each morning, remained a mystery. But regardless of the weather, you could always count on seeing her cheery, red face as she joined the procession down to the river.

With her empty pail trailing, Kei-A-I would wave enthusiastically and call out to each neighbor by name. Then buzzing quickly from woman to woman, she would extract a reluctant greeting and other minor pleasantries. In this childlike way, she sought companionship with the others, unknowingly creating a growing resentment among them.

At this early hour, while the sun rose slowly over the mountains and the northern breezes bit, stung, and nipped at their hands and faces, many of her neighbors were in no mood to be cheerful. But Kei-A-I in her friendly, rasping voice insisted on exchanging cordial greetings and on getting responses from everyone she caught along the way.

Since Kei-A-I made this her daily routine, many women did their best to avoid her. Some chose to stay inside their tepees until Kei-A-I had made the trip. Others, more clever or perhaps more determined, rose much earlier, completed their task quickly, and returned home. But most of the women, despite efforts to evade her, had to endure this cold morning encounter. It was not only Kei-A-I's inexhaustible exuberance or her pestering habit of talking endlessly which upset the tribal women but her dirty, unpleasant appearance.

Kei-A-I would rattle on about everything: the morning, the weather, friends or family. She gossiped about everyone. Some of what she said was fact. Some was what she had heard, but mostly she was given to creating rumors. Her voice was irritating like the high-pitched buzzing sound of insects. Adding to this, her body odor was unbearable. There was a time when some of the women had tried to clean her by giving her a bath and new clothes, but it didn't work. Kei-A-I soon returned to her old ways.

Having prepared, served, and taken part in the morning meal, the women went about their other daily duties. While the men went out to hunt, fish, or craft pottery, the women worked around the campsite. If a woman had young children, her daily chores were usually multiplied. Often another woman would come to help her. Sometimes it would be a mother-in-law; other times a sister or perhaps a grown daughter.

Among the many tasks the women performed was the grinding of the corn into flour. Many of the women would sit just outside their tepee and grind away for hours with a basket of dried corn, a grinding stone, and some water. Occasionally, a nearby neighbor would walk over to work alongside her friend. Not only did this aid in passing the time, but it gave both women a chance to exchange news or small talk concerning their growing families.

These small grinding groups soon became a daily custom among the camp women and did not go unnoticed by the alert Kei-A-I. With a dedication seldom found in others, she began making rounds of these milling circles. Throughout the day, you could see her crossing and recrossing the camp seeking conversation. Whether invited or not, the old woman made herself available to the least bit of information from anyone concerning any member of the tribe. Most women upon whom she intruded did not have the heart to tell her to leave.

There were many reasons why one did not chase a visitor away. Primarily, it was not polite. Just because Kei-A-I was not tactful herself was no reason to double the rudeness. A second reason concerned the tribal custom of treating older members of the tribe with respect. Tribal members did not ever offend elders by rebuking them. Another reason was simply because it would hurt Kei-A-I's feelings, which might bring bad luck to the offender's family. For Kei-A-I was considered touched, lightheaded, or crazy, and crazy people were considered under the special protection of the Great Spirit.

While the milling circles traded family anecdotes, Kei-A-I listened intently. Invariably, as she visited, she took to randomly nibbling and tasting foods which happened to be left about. No one said a word if the old woman helped herself to some leftover portion of a meal. It just wasn't done. As a consequence, as Kei-A-I poked and prodded around, her unsuspecting but polite hostess lost many an exposed meal. In short, if one could stand her odor, a lost meal was nothing.

It went without saying that family gossip, often private, sometimes controversial, and most likely embarrassing was related in the strictest confidence. To divulge any portion of what was heard in these groups to anyone else was considered discourteous. This unwritten code of domestic law did not present any obstacle to Kei-A-I. What she heard was just what she needed to obtain another free meal somewhere else. Everything she learned or overheard was quickly whispered by her into someone else's waiting ear.

It did not take long for everyone in the camp to become aware of Kei-A-I's wagging tongue. When it came to causing trouble, she had no equal. Her creative gossip was only matched by her appetite. Her ability to know that a meal was being prepared became legendary. So too, became her way of visiting those who were in the process of preparing it.

Kei-A-I's most disquieting habit was to appear unannounced, where she was not welcome. She would slip into a tepee and sit down for conversation before her unsuspecting neighbor knew it. Once inside, however, her patient hostess had to hear what Kei-A-I had learned even if she wasn't a bit interested. This breach of confidence by Kei-A-I of telling her neighbors what their relations or friends had disclosed about them made many tribespeople angry at their own kinfolk. After a visit by Kei-A-I, there would often take place an angry exchange between once good friends. Because of the growing communal bickering, arguing, and fighting, the chief believed that more intense feuding would soon take place, unless something were done to stop it.

Kei-A-I was an irritating old woman. There was little doubt of that. Yet, despite all the vengeful rumblings in the camp, life went on. Many of the women, mistrustful of their visitor, learned to be quiet when she was near. They avoided direct conversation with her, and cautious women would bury themselves in their chores. This proved to be an effective excuse. If it wasn't the noonday meal which needed to be made or the clothes which had to be mended, there was always the evening meal to prepare. If these tasks were not enough, there were always short treks to the nearby hills to pick berries, herbs, or to gather nuts.

When darkness veiled the Ndee camp and fires painted the night sky, the tribe settled down to relax in the cool of the evening. However, even the obstacle of darkness did not deter Kei-A-I from roaming between the tepees. This prevented many families from enjoying an evening meal outside their tepee. The more patient reminded the rest that Kei-A-I would eventually learn not to intrude upon others. Others said that someone would finally have enough of her meddling and shoo her away.

But even as the women dreamed of being rid of their unwanted visitor, with the rising sun, she would be there, as cheerful as ever. The men of the tribe, when told of her interference, wondered how she had ever become so nosy. They wanted to do something to relieve their womenfolk, but they couldn't think of an appropriate solution. Unable to circumvent tribal rules, they hoped that someday the chief would be forced to drive her from the camp. This was shortly before the early great winter storm that came in the fall of the year of the White Moon.

With the year's end approaching, and heavy rains commencing a little earlier than usual, everyone in the tribe began to store food for the hard times to come. Kei-A-I, of course, felt that this did not include her. Then, snow struck the upper mountains, causing the women of the tribe to redouble their collective efforts, while the men hastened to dry and cure ample supplies of meat, fish, and furs. Everything was being made ready for the months ahead. No one had time to gossip with Kei-A-I. Instead they warned her of the approaching danger and suggested that she prepare her tepee and help in the communal effort. Kei-A-I smiled, but ignored their advice.

Shortly before the snow fell, the early-rising women, in their haste to prepare for the bad weather, completely disregarded Kei-A-I's morning greetings. Most told her they were in a hurry; others suggested she return another time, because they were too busy to gossip. This made the old woman very sad. Rebuffed for the first time, Kei-A-I made her way home amid the harsh winds, feeling lonely and friendless. She promised herself that one day people would be unable to ignore her. Soon after, the heavy snows of the White Moon hit hard and little was heard from the vexing visitor.

Winter descended upon the camp with an unmistakable fury, and the people who had prepared were glad of their efforts. Inside their tepees, they ignored the freezing winds. Fully protected, the children admired their parents for their wisdom. Throughout the camp, the snug and warm families lay sleeping, while outside their homes, the icy winds snarled angrily. On one particular stormy night, the sky became as black as death and drove so hard, it tore away one unprepared tent, and sent it into the darkness.

It was a cruel winter as many had anticipated. The blizzards were intensely violent and frigid. As time went on, the snows slowly crept up the sides of the sturdy tepees. For those prepared for the tempest, their reward was safety and comfort. With food, wood, and water, there was little to do except wait for the winter to pass.

It was later recalled by the tribespeople that only one winter night was unusually memorable. On that night, some claimed to have heard a cry of despair at their door, which caused them to suspect that someone was out in the blizzard. Since no one risked an investigation, they concluded it was nothing more than the wind imitating the sounds of a woman in agony. For no one unprotected, they agreed, could have survived the winter of the White Moon.

Finally, the spring arrived and so, too, the warming rays of the sun. In reverence for the greening earth appearing through the remaining patches of snow, the tribe named it the year of the Snow Blossom. The green time had returned and everyone rejoiced. The people decided that the first thing to do was to give thanks to the Great Spirit with a spring festival.

Up into the mountains the men went to hunt, while the women set about gathering spring greens and roots. Even the children, when not playing in the meadows, pitched in to help. Days of labor, during which the tribe worked continuously, produced an ample supply of food for the first celebration of the year. While they worked, the women visited undisturbed with one another. These visits produced such harmony and goodwill that eventually some began to wonder what was missing. Then, it struck them. The irritating, nosy visitor was absent.

Kei-A-I was missing and she had not been seen by anyone. None of her neighbors or members of the milling circles had knowledge of her whereabouts. It felt strange to make the morning water trek free from her annoying cheerfulness. Soon people began to wonder what had happened to Kei-A-I. When no one could locate her, they began a camp-wide search. At length, it was concluded that the irksome visitor and her tepee had both completely vanished.

The disappearance of Kei-A-I was believed to be the work of the Great Spirit. He often allowed souls to depart mysteriously. The majority of the women were glad that she would never bother them again. At the same time, they hoped that her kind spirit would find peace. A few even admitted they would miss Kei-A-I's meddling and suggested that the tribe give her a funeral. As they prayed for her, they asked the Great Spirit to find a place for her in his service.

In the spring celebration which followed, the men displayed their finest colored paints, the women their embroidered finery, and the children put on colorful regalia. To the beat of booming drums, they sang and danced for hours. As morning gave way to noon, some continued the dances, while others decided to rest and enjoy the food.

The delicacies of the feast created a pleasing aroma which whet the appetites of everyone. Once served, they began to eat. Some ate alone, others in groups, but wherever they sat, they were soon joined by an unexpected noise. A pesky insect began whizzing and buzzing about their heads as though it was attempting to converse with them. Then it landed, nibbled a bit, drank a bit, then went about sampling every kind of food that was present. Some tried to protect their meal and ignore the troublesome insect, but, in the end, the victim would throw the soiled piece of food away, whereupon the greedy flying pest would have it all to itself.

After the celebration, the persistent insect still hovered over the heads of the women as if trying to get their attention. Failing to do so, it tried to land on them. But they all responded by trying to swat it or shoo it away. Sensing it was not welcome, it invaded the leftovers and began eating again. One of the women sniffing about, asked the others if they detected any new odors. A number of them responded that they did smell something like old, dirty clothes or an unwashed body. Whatever the source, they agreed, it had arrived at the same time as the pesky flying invader.

Taking a closer look at the feeding insect, they noticed that its weblike wings resembled the tattered clothes of their departed Kei-A-I. They quickly realized that her spirit had come back. Soon, everyone was relating observations on the vexing visitor. They remarked how the fly, as they now called her, always seemed to arrive at mealtime. Some described how hard the fly seemed to be trying to speak to them, but no one could make out the buzzing sounds. Eventually, the whole tribe became convinced that their gossipy visitor had returned. It was impossible to ignore her presence. Kei-A-I had been granted her last wish.

Today, among the Apache and other plains tribes, you may see them do a curious thing at mealtime. They will take a tiny bit of food from their plates and put it to one side. In this manner, they remember their departed spirits and the memory of an overly friendly visitor.

Legend of the Flower Maiden

(The Butterfly)

There have been more than a thousand snows in the land of the Apache. This once vast area, which today is sectioned off into reservations in various states, was home to my people. Here in the southwestern plains, an abundance of prairie life and a host of pastoral creatures can be seen. Among them resides a most majestic and independent spirit whose return is awaited and remembered in this spring-told story. To the Apache, it is more than a story: it is a sacred and honored tradition which they use to guide children in the role of obligation. It is known as the song of the Flower Maiden.

Once, long ago, a young Apache girl named Yu-Ti, which means beautiful maiden, was the first born child to the wife of the tribal medicine man. Being the firstborn of this very important couple, she was given special responsibilities. As a girl, Yu-Ti possessed all the gifts and talents sought after in a bride. She excelled at cooking and sewing, and was by far the loveliest maiden in the tribe. Throughout the camp, there were dozens of eager braves who sought to win Yu-Ti's favor. But few suitors compared with the tribe's two favorites.

The first was named Ko-So-Wa, which means hidden love. He was full of vigor, fast in running, climbing, and swimming. With any assortment of weapons, he was recognized as a powerful fighter. His parents were proud of their warrior son. As a hunter and trapper, few could match his skill. His ambition was to marry Yu-Ti, the girl he had loved since childhood.

The second was To-Mo-Ka, which means iron courage. He was a powerful warrior, hunter, and trapper. Although he was not as handsome as Ko-So-Wa, he was good-looking and got many admiring stares from the women who longed to be his chosen one. As for his courage, a great timber wolf had once invaded the Ndee camp and was on the verge of killing a small child when To-Mo-Ka attacked the beast and beat him back in a savage confrontation. This act won for To-Mo-Ka the admiration of the tribe. His aim in life was to win the hand of the loveliest girl in the camp and to that end he would not rest. Many of the people considered him a worthy candidate.

Yu-Ti, being the daughter of the medicine man, was not considered an ordinary woman, free to marry just any brave. Indeed, her husband was to be chosen from among the champions of the tribe in a special contest held to select a new chief. Whoever won the contest also won the hand of the medicine man's daughter. Thus Yu-Ti was obliged to marry the winner for the good of the tribe. The contest showed that the winner possessed special qualities that would lead the people to a safe and prosperous future. Therefore, the people prayed to the Great Spirit to oversee this difficult contest.

In the series of tests, the Great Spirit chose one man above others and then joined him with the first born daughter of the medicine chief. In this way, the chosen of the Great Spirit would be married to the chosen of the people. In the ensuing years, the favor of the Great Spirit would be seen through the union of this couple -- a couple which would always link the people with the Sky Father.

Since Yu-Ti was the firstborn, she was not allowed to marry as her heart desired. Other girls' marriages were simpler. If a young brave wanted to marry an Indian maiden, he had to win her by demonstrating to her father that he was a brave warrior and a good provider. To prove this, he would bring gifts to her father to buy her. Sometimes he brought woven baskets filled with dried corn, meat, or fish. Or he might present the father with a fine pony or rare furs. Of course, there was always the possibility that the father would refuse the gifts, in which case, the bridegroom had to improve his offerings or change his wedding plans.

But, it could not be so for Yu-Ti. She had to marry according to custom, and the custom was that she must marry the superior man. Although love was a great consideration between maid and warrior, it had to give way to tribal law. If the girl found love in the joining, she was considered lucky. If not, it would be bad luck to show her disfavor. She was told by her parents that she could learn to love a great man and more often than not, it turned out that way. For Yu-Ti there was a good chance that her chosen husband would also be her choice as well. Ko-So-Wa was prepared to give his life for her and so was To-Mo-Ka.

On the first day of the new moon, during the celebration of the harvest, the announcement was made that a husband for Yu-Ti would be sought. Every brave had waited a long time to hear those words. Each of them would be given a chance to win the most beautiful woman in the tribe, and to become the new chief. In their most decorative and colorful regalia, the young men gathered in the center of the camp. There they heard the words of the old chief.

"The day of choosing has come! Today these young braves will join together in trial, each one trying to prove himself the chosen one. In this way, our traditions will continue to our children. As it was before our time, so it shall be when we are no more. Let the contest begin!"

The first trial was the running test in which a brave was required to chase after a wild horse on foot and bring him back to camp. This sometimes took several days and so much endurance that many were beaten by the swiftness of the horse. After two days, both Ko-So-Wa and To-Mo-Ka brought their struggling ponies back into camp.

In the second trial the brave had to challenge a swift-flowing river by swimming to its deepest part and retrieving a certain colored stone from the bottom. Many braves nearly drowned while attempting to complete this task, and the few who were successful included the two favorites. With smiles on their faces they stood dripping proudly before the judges, holding out the required stone.

The third trial was one of ingenuity and cleverness. A brave had to go out into the woods with only one arrow and his bow, and then come back with a hunting prize that would feed a family. Since it was a time of moving herds, game was scarce and difficult to find. After a week's trial, only Ko-So-Wa and To-Mo-Ka returned with a large stag apiece. Thus, after the first phase of the trials, it looked as though the choice for a new chief would be between these two champions.

The second phase of the trials soon began and both Ko-So-Wa and To-Mo-Ka looked forward to it. In the next contest each brave was required to defend himself against several opponents at once. Although the opponents were armed with war clubs, the lone brave was not. Still, he had to win without being armed himself. Despite some of the contestants being badly hurt, none was ever killed. To-Mo-Ka and Ko-So-Wa each successfully disarmed their adversaries and stood ready for the final test.

At the same time, Yu-Ti prepared her bridal dress and the tribe prepared for a great celebration. In her soul, she hoped that Ko-So-Wa would win as she loved him deeply. However, should To-Mo-Ka prevail, she would bury her feelings and give herself gladly to the chosen one. Yu-Ti, like many other girls, admired To-Mo-Ka and felt that he was indeed a great warrior. She held no ill feelings toward him. In fact, in her heart, which belonged to Ko-So-Wa, there was a great warmth also for this proud and gentle champion.

The final trial was called the Gift of the Sky Father. It was considered the most important. Each brave having proved himself in the earlier trials was obliged to go to the Spirit Mountain and return with a spirit prize, which would be given to the medicine chief in exchange for the bride. In times past, such prizes as an eagle or the body of a great bear had been judged appropriate. One time, an aspiring brave had captured a herd of mountain sheep. Such gifts were rare and considered to be awarded only by the Giver of Life himself.

The two remaining youths began their journey to the mountain, while the tribe prayed that one would be granted a blessing by the Great Spirit. For many days and nights Yu-Ti's heart was heavy. Then, Ko-So-Wa returned with a majestic gift. Within the circle of the tribe, Ko-So-Wa opened a strange bundle and presented the tribe with a wondrous, magical creature, a baby white buffalo. Truly he had been blessed.

The cheers of the tribe went up in a joyous cry. In their midst was a sacred animal which they believed would give them protection against any enemy. For many in the tribe, the choice for Yu-Ti had been made, and for the beautiful maiden there was only joy in her heart. But others awaited the return of their own favorite.

Several days later, To-Mo-Ka returned and the people were anxious to see what the Great Spirit had granted him. He walked into the camp and everyone gathered to see his gift to the people. Many were surprised when the youth uncovered a colorfully painted drum. They doubted that such a gift was worthy of Yu-Ti. Even the chief and the medicine man thought that Ko-So-Wa was clearly the winner.

"I spoke with the Great Spirit!" proclaimed To-Mo-Ka as many began to walk away disappointed. "As many of you know full well, there are many seasons which we are losing to the winds. Our crops, which wither and die, will no more be given the tears of our women. From this day forward, we shall be blessed with rain."

"How can it be that we will always have rain?" asked the chief.

"We have always had dry seasons," added the medicine man.

"No more!" finished To-Mo-Ka. "From this day onward, our fields will taste the sweetness of the sky."

With every face still showing much disbelief, To-Mo-Ka took from a small pouch a brightly painted drumstick, sat down, and began to beat a slow cadence on his magical drum. Almost as soon as he began to chant, it began to rain. The tribe was astonished! Forever after, their fields would be lush and green and, in turn, the tribe would reap the harvests of the earth. There was no doubt in the minds of the people. These two had both been blessed by the hand of God. But the problem still remained. Which one would be given the hand of their precious Yu-Ti? There seemed to be no way of deciding. Fate decreed that the choice be made by another tribe.

Savage invaders to the north of their peaceful valley were trying to conquer the more civilized tribes. Everywhere these invaders went people were left homeless. They gave no mercy and seldom expected any in return. They were on the warpath and nothing seemed to stop them. Now they became the problem of the Ndee. Their choice was clear, they could stand and fight or they could become one of the conquered peoples. The Apache leader chose to fight.

Yu-Ti, and all the other women who had expected to be married during the celebration, now had to wait as their men painted themselves and dressed for war. The chief, on his horse and in his most decorative array, took the lead and with all his warriors behind him, set out to battle the invader. Among the hundreds of warriors following him were the two camp favorites, who would continue their bid for Yu-Ti once the war was over.

In the following days, weeks, and months, many difficult battles were fought. Great numbers of the enemy were slain, yet it seemed that their numbers were inexhaustible. Eventually, the Ndee, having the power of the white buffalo, gained the final victory. Those of the enemy who survived sued for and were granted a treaty. After a strenuous campaign, the Apache leader returned home where he and his warriors were met with joy, praise, and celebration.

Yet, with the proud victory went sorrow for the many dead. Even the chief had trouble remembering how many battles he had won or how many warriors he had lost. His only consolation was in knowing that the enemy had lost many hundreds more. Great were the stories of bravery that were told. Many were the tales of courage, honor, and self-sacrifice. But alas, in the final counting of the dead, Yu-Ti learned to her horror that her beloved Ko-So-Wa had given his life so that another might live.

Yu-Ti was crushed, realizing that the war had made the choice for her. Her torn heart, although in deep despair, wondered if she would ever love To-Mo-Ka as much as Ko-So-Wa. However, the fates in her life were more cruel than she supposed. Listed among the honored dead was also To-Mo-Ka. Ironically, he had given his life while trying to save Ko-So-Wa. In the following days, the camp was full of wailing cries of sorrow and weeping which accompanied dozens of funeral fires. But the greatest sadness of all was in the heart of Yu-Ti, who felt she had lost the one chance in her life to be truly happy.

Despite their victory, the Ndee remained sad. They all loved Yu-Ti and shared her sorrow. Her constant tears never seemed to have an end and it became difficult for anyone to console her. The nights were long and her unhappiness increased with each rising sun. Finally, she told her people that she would not rest or return until the bodies of the two men were found and given a proper burial.

Her people understood and watched as Yu-Ti set out on her quest. Yu-Ti spent many weeks visiting all the battle sites which the chief had mapped out for her. Day after day, Yu-Ti wandered from battle site to battle site, checking everywhere for the slain warriors. The cold days of autumn increased in number and Yu-Ti began to wonder if she would ever find them. Still she persisted until, at last, tired and exhausted, she fell down. Helpless and utterly lost, she prayed to the Great Spirit for guidance.

"Oh Great Father!" Yu-Ti cried in tears. "Hear the cry of one of your children on the vast land which is watched over by your eyes! Help me great one, help me find the resting place of two of your sons, who were killed in battle! Please grant me the gift of finding their lost spirits!"

"I have watched over your search for days, my daughter," the Sky Father told her. "I am sad when my children make war on each other. I allowed the northern people the power of unity, but they have used it unwisely. Now, they are scattered. As for your tribe, it was not my wish that both your promised ones should be killed. Yet, as I touched them, I touched others as well. For many days I witnessed the sight of their bloodstained bodies draping the land. So terrible was it, that I covered their bodies with soil and grass and now silence grows where they fought and died."

"Then I will never find them again!" cried Yu-Ti in despair. "I shall never be able to learn where they fell and died!"

The Great Spirit was moved by Yu-Ti's tears and decided to give her a chance to find her lost ones.

"So many were the valiant spirits which I lifted into the sky on the days of battle, that I never noticed which brave was which. They were all my sons," explained the Sky Father. "Yet, each warrior who went into battle had his own particular color and design on his shield. I know you will be able to recognize the two you seek if you could see them again. Therefore, I hereby order the ground to yield up its hidden colors and brilliant patterns so that you may inspect them. Henceforth, my daughter, each shield design will display itself in the form of flowers."

The Great Spirit realized that Yu-Ti would never live long enough to search out every battlefield. One lifetime would not be enough. And so, after he commanded the flowers to appear throughout the land, he granted Yu-Ti the power of flight and transformed her into a beautiful butterfly. Each year, her spirit returned with the spring to search and wander among the flowers for her beloved warriors. Amid the flowers the Ndee would see Yu-Ti dancing in the breeze.

Today, Yu-Ti, in her quiet way, still travels from field to field in a continuing search. In remembrance of that endless quest, the Apache honor her with this legend which tells the story of the first butterfly. Each spring, one can see Yu-Ti dancing gently above each flower in a loving search which only the Apache understand. Perhaps someday she will find them.

Legend of the Thunder Wish

(The Buffalo)

There was a time when an invisible hand fathered the great Kansan Sea. As far as the eye could measure, there lay before the viewer an ocean of thick waving grass. This was part of the land of the ancient Ndee--a vast fertile plain that stretched a thousand miles and knew no other inhabitants. One day, according to legend, a man ventured into this sea of tranquility and discovered a treasure which forever enriched the lives of his people.

Wandering Shadow was an old man, an advisor who sat on the tribal council with the other elders. He had lived a good life and had been of great benefit to his people. Still, he felt that a greater destiny awaited him. His people were plainsmen who searched the land for their food. They were religious and devoutly honored the Giver of Life. It was he, they believed, who provided the waters from the sky and the soil of the earth. From the streams and rivers he brought forth fish, and otter and beaver pelts. In the dark forests and mountains, he had taught them to hunt the great cat and the cave bear. To accomplish this, he endowed the Ndee with courage. Because the Great Spirit did so much for them, they often sang praises to him. When he saw that they were happy and grateful, he blessed them further with other special gifts. This is the story of a legendary gift called the Thunder Wish.

It had been a fruitless spring and the severe winter had lingered far longer than the Ndee had prepared for. As a result, their dwindling food supply diminished to meager proportions. In order to provide for their hungry families, the hunters extended their hunting range farther and farther each day. But wherever they journeyed, they found only emptiness. Not surprisingly, when they returned empty handed, the tribe became increasingly despondent. There was nothing to hunt, the warriors explained. The snowy plains were barren of game, and the rivers were devoid of life.

Except for the children, the tribe went days at a time without eating. The effects were immediate. At the end of the first month, the people began counting their sick. After the second, their dead. By the third month, the chief was pressed to do something. He had to decide whether to stay and wait for the snow geese, deer, and other seasonal animals to return or journey southward.

His advisors explained that traveling at this time would be risky. If they moved, they might find only vacant waste- land. Further, if they went too far, they might never return. On the other hand, if they did not do something, the contin- uing bad weather would subject the rest of the tribe to certain death by starvation.

The chief and his council discussed these two alarming possibilities at great length with neither choice being ac- cepted. Some argued that the unknown desert lands to the south needed proper reconnaissance first, adding that such efforts would require time and use up their best warriors. Time, explained the chief, was their main problem. So whatever was to be decided, he had to choose soon, before the weather made the choice for him. One elder expressed concern for the children who would not be able to make any journey without nourishment. The chief and his council finally agreed, there had to be another alternative.

Something had to be done; his people depended on him. The chief decided to consult with the medicine man. The Great Spirit must be angry reasoned the chief, or else why would the winter be so severe. The chief asked the medicine man to visit the Spirit Mountain to pray to their Sky Father for assistance. The final decision would rest on the outcome of the medicine man's quest.

A few days later, the medicine man returned from the Spirit Mountain and went to the chief's tepee, saying he had discovered why the spring had not replaced the winter. This was what the chief was waiting to learn. Gathering the elders, the chief told them to sit and listen to what the Great Spirit had advised.

The Great Spirit, explained the shaman, was not angry at all. He simply was not at home among the clouds as he had always been. The Great One had gone searching for one of his special possessions. This was why there was no change in the weather. The tribe had to help the Great Spirit in his search, the medicine man added, or else the cold would continue and destroy everything. The sooner the Great Spirit recovered his lost possession, the sooner the Ndee would regain their strength.

Knowing the cause of their misery, the chief ordered all his warriors out in all directions to search for the lost possession. When someone asked what it was they were seeking, the chief replied that when they found it, they would know it belonged in the sky. The entire tribe rose weakly the following day to wish success to their men. Among those who did not go were the women, the young, the sick, and the very old. However, even though he was not required to join the searchers, Wandering Shadow insisted on going too. Although many suggested he should not, he nevertheless felt compelled to aid in the search. Bundling up warmly, he set out across the empty plain. Not much later, he became completely lost.

The open prairie of the Kansan Sea had limits, but no one knew its actual size. To a novice traveler, it could prove overwhelming. In his youth, Wandering Shadow had explored much of the plain, always feeling that he was the first to do so. Regardless of how often he journeyed out, he was always certain of his location. His father had taught him how to use the stars and the rising sun at daybreak to learn his position. However, now, in a blinding blizzard neither aid was available. Still the old warrior was unafraid, for he felt something near urging him on.

The snow had thoroughly blanketed the horizon with a heavy white shroud, which, despite its brightness, produced a gloomy quality, making it difficult to see. With an imaginary fixed point in the distance, Wandering Shadow trudged forward. On and on he walked, his determination to find the lost object providing his strength. Someone had to find the lost possession. Failure would mean disaster for his people.

After what seemed like an indeterminable amount of time, the old man stopped, sat down crushing the snow beneath him, and looked for his trail. His heart sank when he realized that beyond the last few steps, there were none! His breathing became erratic, imitating a clogged flow of steam. If he was to continue like this, he would never make it back to the camp. There was little food in his pouch but plenty of water, although it was beginning to freeze, as was his blood pumping through his veins. It took him a great effort to rise again but he prevailed. After a few steps, he heard a distant cry.

Stopping for a moment, Wandering Shadow listened intently. His lungs burned inside him from gasping the freezing air. Seconds later, he heard the noise again. It sounded like a moan coming from someone in pain. Using the sound as a guide, he walked toward it. His heart began pounding like a great war drum. He felt exhausted and somewhat dizzy. Stopping again, he peered through the hazy white curtain toward a murky glittering object. There, a dozen yards away, he saw something lying in the snow. Rushing forward, he came upon a strange man buried neatly in the drift. Without hesitating, Wandering Shadow began digging until the man was free.

The stranger lay unconscious in a glittering blue and black jeweled blanket. It shimmered brightly against the snowy landscape. Wandering Shadow had never seen such garments as the man wore. They were not made of animal skins or reeds but a curious blend of metals. Building a fire to warm him, the old man studied the man intently. The stranger was not of the Ndee tribe, of that he was sure. Further, he did not wear markings which identified him with members of any other particular tribe; rather he wore them all! The man's face was unusually painted with unfamiliar patterns. As Wandering Shadow continued to gaze at him, he concluded he was not of the Plains Tribes. Perhaps, he was from the east.

The stranger's physique was unusual too. He was much taller than men of Wandering Shadow's tribe. He was tan in complexion, large and quite heavy, but not fat. His hair was braided and silver-gray. It was textured like fine threads in a web. His muscular face gave the impression that it had been carved from stone. What bothered Wandering Shadow was that he did not possess any weapons nor appear to be a weakling. Quite the opposite, he suspected the stranger would have little difficulty killing a full-grown bear with his bare hands. So what was he doing in the snow?

Two hours after Wandering Shadow had discovered him, the stranger awoke and immediately asked for something to drink. The old man obliged him, offering his water bag and curious that the stranger could speak the Ndee language. With a surprising thirst, the stranger drained the container, then abruptly asked for food. Without hesitation, Wandering Shadow gave him what little he had, and then sat back and watched the strange man devour it.

Upon completing the meager meal, the stranger stood and stretched lazily. From this action Wandering Shadow concluded without doubt that the stranger was no ordinary brave, but a warrior of extraordinary proportions. Without saying a word, the stranger warmed himself, then walked away from the campfire and disappeared into the brilliant whiteness of the plain. Wandering Shadow waited a moment, but the man did not return. It was truly the strangest encounter he had ever experienced. Oddly enough, he had not learned the man's name.

There was no bitterness in Wandering Shadow's heart, only a puzzled question as he set out to continue his search. Much later, he was completely exhausted, nearly blind, and extremely hungry. Still, there was no sign of life on the ivory landscape. On the tenth day out, he fell into the soft snow and decided it was a good place to die. Lying resigned, and staring out across the blinding distance, he unexpectedly saw a spiraling pillar of blue smoke rising from the white earth. It was the first time in his life he was confronted by a daytime apparition. Could it be a dream or a mirage, he wondered as he stood and staggered toward it. Whatever it was, it was something to live for.

Although Wandering Shadow was sure that the spiraling smoke was much closer than it appeared, he was wrong. It took him an hour to reach the apparition. As he did, a mysterious sight met his eyes. The source of the column was a hole in the snow. On closer observation, he saw that something lay in the hole just inches beneath the snow line. Curiosity drove him to dig until he touched the object. Then, ever so gently, he lifted it from the ground and held it up.

Wandering Shadow was unsure of what he had discovered, but he was positive of one thing, he had never seen anything like it. The object was a glittering blue pouch tightly laced with a tiny metal string. It resembled a large metal gourd and pulsed with power. Gripping it tightly, Wandering Shadow could feel it vibrating. Perhaps he was in danger. Putting it down, he stepped away. The pouch radiated an invisible aura informing him that he had something which did not belong to an ordinary mortal. He was convinced that he had found the sacred possession of the Great Spirit.

Realizing he had to get it back to his people, Wandering Shadow again took up the pouch, inserted it into his carry bag, and placed it on his shoulder. He then began walking home. Instantly, he sensed he was heading in the wrong direction. Turning about, he walked as though he had had a week's rest and had feasted well before starting out. The gnawing hunger in his belly was replaced with satisfaction. His snow blindness disappeared and he easily spied his camp miles and miles away. He quickly increased his already rapid pace. Within hours he was back in the camp and among his people. He felt proud and most grateful for having survived the blizzard and for having returned home safely.

The people of the tribe were surprised when Wandering Shadow returned unharmed. Nevertheless, they informed him of the murderous storm which had buried the prairie under five feet of snow. It was the storm, they said, which had forced two hundred of their best warriors to be defeated in the quest. Not one of them had any luck in finding the lost article. Since Wandering Shadow looked as though he had not been affected by the blizzard at all, the people did not bother asking him any questions.

As the old man walked through the camp, he saw that things had not improved. His people were still hungry, sick, and in need of a miracle. Appearing from among the gathering crowd, the medicine man told the tribe that he had had a vision. In his dream, he said, the magical pouch belonging to the Great Spirit had been found. Immediately, a great cry of joy went up from the crowd. Wandering Shadow then unexpectedly interrupted the joyous cheering, proclaiming that he had met the Great Spirit and given him food and drink. Furthermore, he added, he had the magic pouch and wanted to know what to do with it. The people began laughing at Wandering Shadow until he produced the glittering blue object. Instantly, they stopped their jeering and knelt in fear when they saw the great spiral of blue smoke come from the pouch.

The Great Spirit, explained the medicine man, had fought with a storm giant and during their battle, he had lost the pouch. As a result, the Great Spirit's powers were weakened and he fell to the earth below. There he remained for several days until a Ndee tribesman had chanced upon him. Wandering Shadow, he related proudly, was telling the truth. Because of his kindness to the Great Spirit, he was to be rewarded. Everyone then apologized and openly praised the aging warrior.

Continuing to relate his dream, the medicine man explained how the pouch should be returned. After the medicine man told him where to take the magical pouch, Wandering Shadow immediately set off for the Spirit Mountain. There, the Great Spirit accepted his possession and offered the old man anything he wished. Wandering Shadow replied that he would like to consult with his people, since he planned to share it with them. The Great Spirit understood and allowed him to return.

When Wandering Shadow told his people he had returned the pouch, they were pleased. In gratitude, he explained, the Great Spirit had offered him anything he wanted. But he was not certain what was needed most, and thus he sought advice from the tribe. "What should I ask for?" he inquired. Instantly, a hundred voices began shouting. The tribe went wild with suggestions. The air was smothered with requests, advice, appeals, and demands. "We need food!" appealed one. "We need clothes!" advised another. "Weapons!" added a third. "Tools!" cried a fourth. "Grant us peace!" suggested the elders. "No, blankets! Trading goods! Jewelry! Medicine! Power! Strength! Health! Rain! Sunlight! The spring! The summer! Water! Crops!" On and on it continued.

For several riotous moments, hundreds and hundreds of screaming voices raged loudly over each other. Finally, the chief asked for and received silence. "He has but one wish," he reminded them. "If it is to be shared, let all share it." Silence followed his statement. "What is needed most?" he asked seriously. When no one offered an answer, he decided the council should make the choice. Yet, despite a night's debate, the council could not agree on anything.

Because the tribal council was unable to reach an agreement over what should be asked for, the people were disappointed. Dozens of fights broke out. Disunity and discontentment added to everyone's woes, filling Wandering Shadow with sorrow. Sadly, he left his bickering people and went back to the Spirit Mountain, where he related the problem to the Great Spirit. "Earthly treasures are often clouded by rampant desires," remarked the Great Spirit. "Tell me what your people need and I will decide." Wandering Shadow repeated the long list. "And what is your desire?" the Great Spirit asked. "Wisdom, Great Father," he replied. "Allow me to prevail against myself and my enemies." "Return then," finished the Great Spirit. "You shall have it."

Deep in thought, Wandering Shadow pondered upon how the Great Spirit would solve the complex problem of which option the tribe needed most. Failure to select the right one would cause many in the tribe to be resentful and angry. But with this puzzling question came a comforting thought; if anyone ever exercised wisdom, the Great Spirit did. When he next appeared in the camp, Wandering Shadow was surrounded and showered with dozens of greetings.

They thanked Wandering Shadow for the unique opportunity of sharing his wish, but they agreed that by themselves they could not be sure of adopting the best choice. They were certain that the aging councilman, with his wisdom, would choose rightly for them all. They were disappointed to learn, however, that he too was unwilling to chance the wrong wish. Then Wandering Shadow told them that he had requested the Great Spirit to select something for all. The tribe cheered and praised him for his sound judgment. Whatever the Great Spirit decided was sure to bear approval, because they had never quarreled over any of his previous gifts.

Walking home that night, the people talked about their fondness for Wandering Shadow. The famed elder had mentioned everyone's request. Now it remained to be seen which one the Great Spirit would pick. That night Wandering Shadow had a strange dream. In his vision, his gift was providing the mainstay of his people. An annual ceremony would mark its arrival. Its power would make his people invincible.

The following day, the landscape had completely altered. The snow had vanished and the cold had disappeared. Shining brightly, the sun illuminated the plains as far as the eye could see. The sky was a deep blue and fluffy clouds patched the ground with shade. The vastness of the prairie rippled with a huge billowing carpet of fresh grass. The nearby forests were teeming with life. Birds flew and sang, while fish sported in the streams. Game of every sort was seen grazing in the hills and mountains. The fragrance of spring flowers filled the tribe with a zest for life, and they were grateful to be alive. Was this the gift of the Great Spirit? They wondered. Wandering Shadow assured them, it was not. Their gift would arrive in two nights and would be under their control. Speculations abounded on what he meant.

The Ndee waited eagerly and anxiously for a night and day for the gift. Hour by hour, their excitement grew. By nightfall, the restive clan had gathered in the meeting place amid dozens of torchlights. Wandering Shadow worried over their unruly demeanor. Standing atop a mound with many torches illuminating his worried face, Wandering Shadow related to his people his recent dream. "In my vision," he said loudly, "the Great Spirit instructed me to tell you that his gift will make us invincible as long as we honor it. The Great Spirit has named it Ton-Ton-Ka, the Brave One."

With their attention focused on him, Wandering Shadow continued to explain the tribe's special gift. "We must preserve Ton-Ton-Ka in our hearts and songs. From this night onward, we will share his strength. If we break our bond with him, we will not be invincible." "How do we receive Ton-Ton-Ka?" asked the chief. "At this moment, he sleeps within the earth," said Wandering Shadow. "The earth!" echoed many in the great crowd. "It is in the soil that Ton-Ton-Ka lives," explained Wandering Shadow. "Through him, we shall obtain our food, our clothes, our tools, our weapons, our medicine, and the other items we asked for."

"Can we see him?!" inquired the impatient people. "Only if you promise not to frighten him or his family," advised Wandering Shadow. "Failure to heed this will invite danger as well as disaster. If you stay here, I will go alone and bring him back to you."

They nodded their assent and Wandering Shadow went out and entered a huge earthen pit in the prairie. But the crowd was too curious to keep its word and it followed Wandering Shadow. The throng pushed forward into the entrance tearing open the door protecting Ton-Ton-Ka's home. Unaware of their effect, the people burst in with their many voices and fiery torches, creating a disastrous chain of events that few would be able to recall.

No sooner had the unruly mob broken into the massive underground cavern than the earth beneath their feet began to tremble, rumble, and shake, throwing many to the floor. Unfortunately, the ones thrown were also the ones carrying the torches. Darkness immediately added confusion to the existing state of disorder. Panic ensued. Those entering turned around immediately and dashed for the starlit exit, trampling those still pushing their way in.

As the Ndee shot out from the underground pit, on their heels came murderous earsplitting sounds from an unimaginable source. The earth grumbled loudly and pitched uncontrollably. The walls of the cave began to break and crumble inward. Many feared the very planet was breaking in half.

Bursting forth into the still, dark night, the panicking crowd shrieked and dashed for safety. Close behind, the booming roar came into contact with the night air, multiplying in volume and exploding with a terrific force. As the last person escaped, the more courageous or foolishly reckless, turned to observe what emerged behind them.

The earth, amid a massive roar of falling rocks, dust, and debris, was emptying a creature of earthly thunder onto the shadowy plain. The creature, which the stunned tribe saw from a distance, was colossal, yet it continued to increase in size every few seconds. Its mysterious ghostly appearance indicated an animal of gigantic proportions. Its profile was low, rough, and shaggy, and it was covered with a million ivory horns. The woolly creature snorted gruffly through thousands of flaring red nostrils and featured countless fiery eyes. A cavalcade of angry hooves accompanied the phenomenal growth of the creature. In shock, the people watched helplessly as their precious gift thundered unimpeded into the distance, enveloping the prairie like a huge unrolling carpet. The sight would remain in their minds for long afterwards. Whatever it was, they thought, it was gone.

With the night deepening, the chief and his people walked home quietly. Throughout the night they heard the trembling of the earth, which reminded them of their impulsiveness. Hundreds of images filled their dreams as they tried to imagine what it might have been that they saw that night. The following day, the tribe assembled and asked forgiveness of Wandering Shadow and asked if they had truly lost their gift. "The gift remains ours," the old man informed them. "The only thing we have lost is our control over it. From now on, we will have to search for it. If you wish to see it, come with me."

Wandering Shadow took his people to a high promontory overlooking the Kansan Sea. Below them, Ton-Ton-Ka grazed undisturbed. A cry of astonishment erupted from the hearts of the people as they stared across the prairie. There below them, stretching to the far horizon, was not one creature as they had supposed but the most gigantic herd of buffalo in the world. In the years to come, Ton-Ton-Ka would provide the children of the Great Plains invincible power and a wealth of meat, clothing, tools, and weapons from its herds.

For many generations, the Apache kept their pledge and honored Ton-Ton-Ka in their songs. During these centuries they remained unconquered by anyone. In time, however, they forgot their vow. As a result they suffered from many enemies. Although they tried to restore their bond with Ton-Ton-Ka, their invincibility never returned. Today, the descendants of the ancient Ndee, the modern Apache, live in the shadow of their former glory. Ton-Ton-Ka remains a vanishing breed whose former greatness lives only in the memory of the Thunder Wish.

CLEVELAND

Legend of the Endless War

(The Cat and the Dog)

Long before the European first set foot upon the land of the Apache, it contained a stillness which would come to be known as peace and quiet. This calm was a special gift from the Giver of Life, who had bequeathed silence to the prairie. Acknowledging this gift, the Ndee gained a spiritual strength unknown to other men. But their land was not always so peaceful. Once, two feuding tribes nearly destroyed the serenity of the land. Their troublesome saga teaches Apache children the lesson of futility.

Long ago, three plains tribes came into contact with each other. The first was a tribe of fierce mountain fighters called the Stone Children, for it was said they came from the Stone River. These people were wild and savage, and demanded much of life. Though they required much, they returned little. The Stone Children fought incessantly, but they had only one mortal enemy, the Gray Rock people, upon whom they vowed eternal vengeance.

The second tribe were also warriors. These people came from the Gray Basin beyond the horizon, hence their name, the Gray Rock. They too were blessed with many skills, but they suffered from extreme stubbornness. Because of it, they achieved little stability. They allowed themselves to prolong a dispute which should have ended long before. Since they were unaccustomed to accepting blame, they seldom admitted mistakes. Suffice to say, because of their stubbornness, they promised the Stone Children perpetual war as long as they lived.

65

The final tribe was the Ndee. Unlike the first two, they were wise and patient people. It is they who remember the story.

Where the endless war originated remains a mystery. Some believe it began in a peaceful valley near the Yellow River. This gentle channel, whose waters eventually empty into the great Colorado, derived its name from its glittering golden quality. Ancient tribes claimed that the river bottom was layered in gold. Others said it was only goldenrod lining the shore. But, even if it were only the rays of the sun playing upon the flowing stream, it never glittered again after two nomadic tribes discovered the quiet valley.

In the early autumn of the year of the Snow Fox, the Stone Children came down from the mountains and settled on the wooded banks of the Yellow River. In the same month, at nearly the same time, the Gray Rock people took possession of the opposite shore.

At first, the tribes seemed friendly enough. Daily, they went about establishing their respective campsites, paying little attention to one another. But as the season waned, the tribes anticipated that a bitter winter would soon arrive. With that threat in mind, the two tribes began assembling great stores of winter supplies. The men of both camps spent much time trapping, hunting, and fishing before the gales brought the snow. The women, too, prepared for winter. There was much to be done. Aside from making pottery, blankets, and winter clothing, they dried great quantities of meat and fish. Additional time was spent curing all the animal skins. In the course of this mutual endeavor, the Stone people discovered that the Gray Rock clan across the wide river excelled in collecting food. They became envious of their neighbor and contrived to gain his secrets. That was the last day of peace in the valley.

With a brisk wind tossing the first snowflakes about, a Stone tribe envoy crossed the Yellow River and invited his industrious neighbors to an autumn celebration. The Gray Rock people having completed their winter preparations, gladly accepted. But no sooner had the festival begun than the merriment gave way to loud bickering over each tribe's hunting and fishing skills. The Stone Children boasted that no tribe could match them. The Gray Rock people were surprised at such an empty claim. They were convinced their hosts were bragging, and decided to disgrace them by proposing a contest of skills.

The chief of the Stone Children declared that to ensure fairness, his hunters would accompany his guests during their hunts, and that twenty major prizes would be the goal. The Gray Rock chief, unaware of his host's intentions, agreed. With the rules established and the hunting parties selected, the contest began.

Because of their extraordinary skill, the Gray Rock hunters soon tracked and killed the required quota of prey. Although they tried to disguise their methods, the accompanying Stone Children hunters soon discovered their hunting secrets. The Gray Rock hunters begged the Stone Children warriors never to reveal the secrets. Feigning reluctance, the Stones promised to keep the Gray Rock hunters' wishes on the condition that they allow them to keep the trophies. Fearing dishonor, the Gray Rock hunters agreed.

The contest ended with the clever Stone Children acknowledging the Gray Rock clan as better hunters, but they insisted that there were better fishermen. Again the Gray Rocks proved them wrong, but, with the same rules applying, and in order to guard their technique, they allowed the Stone tribe to keep the prizes. The Gray Rocks had won the events, but unwittingly they had provided the Stone Children with enough provisions to last the winter.

Spring arrived and the two tribes were still on friendly terms, so much so that marriages between the tribes were allowed. The Gray Rock people considered this a sign of brotherhood, when in fact the alliance was designed by the Stone Children as a safeguard against the Gray Rock people seeking revenge. Still, the Gray Rock people believed in the peaceful motives of their war prone neighbor.

But peace between the two tribes did not last. One day, a Gray Rock woman accidentally overheard a rude remark made by two women of the Stone tribe. They sarcastically recalled how their chief had duped the Gray Rock tribe in the winter contest. This revelation was soon brought before the Gray Rock council, which, after much inquiry, discovered that they had indeed been tricked. They decided the insult warranted reprisal, and singled out a Stone tribe woman who had been widowed prior to marrying her Gray Rock husband and forcibly returned her to the Stone Children in disgrace. This shame incensed her proud father who demanded that the Gray Rock husband reaccept her on pain of death. The husband not only refused, but he urged his brothers who had recently married Stone wives to do the same as he had done. When this took place, it infuriated the Stone Children.

In response to the outrage, the Stone Children drove their Gray Rock women across the river, but not before beating them severely. This violence incited the Gray Rock tribe to ambush a Stone tribe youth and thrash him to near unconsciousness. Dazed, the boy staggered back to his camp whereupon his people vowed vengeance. Under the cover of darkness, a band of Stone warriors crept into their neighbor's camp and killed a popular Gray Rock brave. This induced the Gray Rock warriors into open war against their deceitful neighbor. From that day onward, they promised no peace until all the Stone Children were dead!

Eight years after the first incident, the two warring tribes had not rested. Although they occasionally met on the open battlefield, most encounters took place near the Yellow River. New violence would begin when the women washing their clothes or cleaning their fish near the river's edge would hurl strings of insults across the river at their neighbors. This exchange of words would be succeeded by a hail of stones. Thereafter, volleys of arrows and spears would follow. This led to brief skirmishes, followed by a full scale battle. The result, each time, was several people dead on both sides of the river.

The number of battles increased and still the war continued. Shortly after the dead had been buried, the crying women would urge their remaining braves to seek vengeance for loved ones killed. The warriors, having more pride than sense, would attack the enemy to avenge these losses. Eventually, the attack would be reciprocated by the defenders.

After ten years, neither side could remember the number of their dead. Their only consolation was in believing the other side had sustained greater losses. Neither tribe ever ran out of reasons for launching yet another reprisal against their enemy. It did not matter that no one could recall the reason for the conflict. They cared only that the other side was to blame.

Surrounding tribes in the immense valley had become accustomed to the endless war. They tried to mediate between the two factions, but time after time, the peace lasted only a few days and was then followed by a new argument at the river's edge, which led to yet another battle. Finally, one tribe, called the Ndee, could no longer endure the constant battle cries, loud war drums, and lamenting women. They decided to send their eldest and wisest medicine man to reconcile the warring tribes. His name was So-Tay-O.

So-Tay-O was an old man. Yet his knowledge, patience, and wisdom surpassed others. His tribe, a simple people, wanted nothing more than peace to return to their land. They hoped So-Tay-O could settle the seemingly endless dispute. With that task in hand, he journeyed to the Yellow River basin.

Upon arriving and walking through their desolated camps, he saw that both sides had lost most of their warriors. Each tribe had suffered greatly from the long war. But despite the devastation, they still maintained hostility toward each other. Regardless, So-Tay-O knew he had to try to bring peace. And try he did. For several weeks, he advised, pleaded, and implored both sides to trust his efforts. Eventually, the chiefs and their respective peoples gathered for a peace talk.

So-Tay-O was surprised to learn that neither side could remember the origin of the war, both sides maintaining that the other had started it. Quickly and before they could begin fighting anew, So-Tay-O argued that no one could benefit from the continued fighting. He pointed out that everyone had already paid heavily for their aggression and should recognize the hopelessness of it.

Reluctantly the two tribes agreed to end the war. However, after promising peace and after Say-Tay-O had returned home, they began accusing each other of dishonesty. What happened next was inevitable. That night the final conflict began, lasting several days and nights. The wail of death reverberated throughout the valley, convincing the Ndee that the two tribes were annihilating one another. Days later the valley became so quiet that So-Tay-O was asked to investigate.

Riding slowly over the vast plain, So-Tay-O listened intently. All about, nature's choir accompanied his journey. Above him in the blue sky, the birds sang their songs, while all about, various small animals added volume to their melody. He smiled as the creatures scampered through the tall grass. In the distance he could hear the rolling thunder of the gentle buffalo crossing the broad expanse. Only one sound was missing: the discord of battle. It was unusually quiet and the old man could only fear the worst.

Arriving above the Yellow River, So-Tay-O gazed down and saw to his horror that both camps lay in smoldering ruins. They seemed devoid of life. There were no men, no women, no children, no goats, no tepees, nothing! The floor of the valley was littered with bodies and smoking debris. The once green valley was shrouded in black ash. Everywhere he turned he saw devastation. The famed golden river was tinged with the redness of blood. Had it not been for his courage, the old man would have departed from the terrible scene.

So-Tay-O spent days burying the dead and cleaning the polluted river banks. Throughout his life, he had never witnessed such brutal carnage. Why had they fought? Neither tribe was ever sure. Now there was no one left. If only they had not destroyed themselves, they might yet have found peace. But now it was too late. With confused thoughts, the old man went about his task. Suddenly he caught a faint cry rising from beneath an ashen pile. So-Tay-O waited a moment, then he heard the sound again. Convinced it was a child, the old man fell near it and dug furiously discovering a bundled baby. Truly this was a miracle. With the child protected, So-Tay-O finished cleaning the Stone tribe area. Much later, while cleaning the Gray Rock camp, he again heard the wail of a hungry baby. With great eagerness So-Tay-O uncovered the second infant, delighted that he could save another life.

It took So-Tay-O a great deal of time to complete his grim task. However, once he finished, he turned his attention to the two infants. The first was a boy from the Stone Children tribe. The medicine man, recalling how he had lifted him from the ashes, called him Gray Ghost. The other was a girl from the Gray Rock tribe. She had large, lunar eyes, so he named her Bright Moon. With the babies in tow, So-Tay-O returned to his people's camp.

The old man arrived exhausted, but nevertheless, he spent an hour explaining to his people what had transpired. Producing the two orphans he had found in the ruins, he described how the two tribes had apparently massacred one another. So-Tay-O believed the orphans could be taught to live in peace as they grew up. This goal, he said, would require the vigilance of everyone. Someday, he added, the Ndee would explain to the orphans how their tribes had destroyed each other. But that lay in the future. For now, the children were given beds in the tepee of an experienced mother, far from the feuding spirits of their tribes.

That night when everyone was asleep, a terrible crying shattered the camp's stillness. The entire tribe rose to see what was causing the noise. Amid the glow of torches, they discovered that the two newcomers were the source of the disturbance. Dozens of mothers offered reasons why the babies cried. But regardless of what was tried, nothing worked to calm their distress. Finally, the chief noticed that the two babies stopped wailing when separated from each other. If brought together, the two would whine excitedly. This was strange, but at his people's request, the keepers of the two babies were ordered to have them sleep in different tepees. Thereafter, the camp returned to bed. For So-Tay-O and his people, this was only the beginning of a new ordeal.

As time passed, the infants never overcame their dislike of being close to one another. When it became apparent that this was a pattern, it was decided the two should be reared in different sections of the camp. Later, as they developed, it was quite evident that they had acquired an irritating aggressiveness. The two were likable enough with other children, but regardless of the gifts they were offered to be tolerant with each other, the two always squabbled. Despite years of patient tutoring, Gray Ghost and Bright Moon were unable to acquire any patience with each other. So-Tay-O tried to teach them the folly of quarreling, but despite his best efforts, and that of his people, he failed. No one could understand why.

Never in the tribe's history had two children been born with such mistrust. The two remained quiet only when So-Tay-O was present. If he left them alone, the pair would be found scratching, biting, kicking, and hurting each other. On many occasions, the tribe sadly observed Gray Ghost chasing his half sister through the camp in an attempt to kill her. It was only her quickness and agility which prevented him from doing so.

At a young age, Gray Ghost began receiving instruction from the men of the tribe in the hope it might mature his attitude. He was taught the value of honor, strength, and courage. These the boy mastered, becoming a credit to his teachers. The warriors taught him to ride, hunt, fish, and trap animals. These skills, too, he acquired. As for Bright Moon, she was schooled in the ways of a woman. By age twelve, she had mastered the skills of sewing, cooking, cleaning, and basket weaving. In every ability required of her, she was an expert. If the two youngsters had any problem, it lay in their lack of love for the other.

By the time the agitating duo had reached their midteens, So-Tay-O and his people had endured years of their bickering. The children aged, but only their features changed. Gray Ghost had become a dark, handsome man with silver eyes and coal-black hair. His half sister had developed into a striking beauty, but with an unpredictable nature which bristled at the sight of her brother. Unlike their physical attributes, their dispositions toward each other had not altered. The two were still bitter rivals.

Unlike So-Tay-O, the tribe had given up on the two, yet they waited to see if their maturity would grant the people some measure of peace. In his manhood, Gray Ghost had studied tolerance, but he never used it on his sister. Bright Moon had learned compassion, but she believed her brother unworthy of it. So-Tay-O repeatedly urged them to reconcile their differences. Despite this, the two remained adamant in their attitudes.

With the ensuing years the dispute which had destroyed their two nations raged on between them. Because they were no longer children, the tribe was unable to prevent them from arguing into the night. Unable to comprehend why the two had never learned to like one another, their aging father, at the request of the tribe, journeyed to the Spirit Mountain to seek the advice of the Great Spirit. In the solitude of the mountain, the old man prayed for days and nights. He asked that his two warring children be given a place to live in peace. He beseeched the Great Spirit to grant his people the quiet of their ancestors. So-Tay-O assured the Great Spirit that his children were good people and begged pity for them. After four days and nights, the medicine man returned to the camp.

Upon arriving, So-Tay-O was informed that the quarrelsome couple had vanished and that quiet had returned to the camp. Was this the work of the Great Spirit, wondered the people. Perhaps, sighed So-Tay-O. Unable to sleep during the following nights, he felt an urge to return to the Yellow River valley. The tribe advised him to forget the bickering pair, but he replied it was a matter of personal importance.

So-Tay-O reached the valley to discover the land renewed and a new tribe settled there. They were a friendly people. As he entered their camp, they made him welcome, offering him food and refreshment. The elders asked if the Eternal One had sent him to them to explain their recent fear. Feeling honored, So-Tay-O said yes, whereupon, the tribe led him to a large bowl-like pasture crescented by a dark forest. On the hillside, they invited him to sit and wait. Curious about their fear, So-Tay-O sat down while the elders spoke to him of two ferocious apparitions which appeared daily, disturbing the quiet and frightening them. Before So-Tay-O could speak, a terrific howling and shrieking exploded from within the forest, petrifying everyone.

Shooting out from the thicket came a sleek, elegant yellow mountain cat. Due to its incredible speed, the old man could not see it clearly. Then briefly, it stopped and looked about, allowing So-Tay-O to closely observe its small sculptured face, where two large, lunar eyes dominated its features. Abruptly, a second figure appeared, causing the cat to streak away. Hot on the cat's heels, sped the enormous silhouette of a handsome black wolf, howling with murderous fury. So-Tay-O instantly recognized the war cry of Gray Ghost.

With the two ghostly figures streaking away, it was difficult to study them. Regardless, So-Tay-O knew the glowing figures were his children, barking, snarling, hissing, and clawing at each other as they had done all their lives. The onlookers inquired if they were demons? So-Tay-O reassured them. The animals were only the first dog and the first cat ever created, and man needed only to tolerate their constant fighting.

For the Ndee, it was the end of a long road, during which they learned that for some tribes, a good war is better than a bad peace. In this case, the Great Spirit had granted the two remnants of two warring peoples all eternity to continue the Endless War--a war remembered in legend by the Apache.

CLEVELAND

Legend of the Black Flame

(The Gila Monster)

*I*n the ages before any European explored the uncharted *regions of the Southwest, this magical story was popular among the Ndee. During the many festivals held to honor the dead, there was one which recalled a special warrior. He had many names, such as Death that is Fire, or Painted Skin, but the most common was Black Flame. The legend of the Black Flame exemplifies what the Apache consider among the most important qualities in a warrior, such as courage, strength, and endurance.*

Overlapping the borders of present day New Mexico and Arizona lies a great expanse of rocky desert, which moderns have christened the Great Gila. According to legend, this vast wilderness was once a beautiful forest containing many natural wonders. The present landscape was not always inhospitable and hostile. Once it held a gigantic lake enclosed by thousands of miles of sloping pine forests and bordering fertile fields. The forest valleys were undisturbed by even the most intensive storms. In this richly blessed area, one thousand Ndee tribesmen lived with their families.

The legend of the Black Flame began in the year of the Dark Sky, and took place in the plain of the Iron Tree. The ancient Ndee were a peaceful people who practiced hunting and who knew the art of healing with herbal medicines. They had lived for generations without the slightest conflict. Indeed, they had no word for war. They were not a greedy people, nor were they quarrelsome. Theirs was a cherished way of life. For nearly all of their history, they had no enemy and did not seek one. But all this was to change.

ring as they did in their beautiful valley, the Ndee
_ jed an uncommon harmony. They experienced little
sickness, no hardship, and most important of all, no hunger. When the men hunted, they seldom returned disappointed. The reason lay in the animal abundance in the
woods, rivers, and hills. The hunters exerted only a modest
effort but always returned with a bounty of food.

The women were examples of serenity. Their daily family
chores were easily accomplished due to the fact that the
young and the old worked together with great communal
accord. Because the families helped one another, the tasks
of mending, cooking, and cleaning were free of strenuous
difficulty. As a result, the entire tribe was always well fed,
clean, and healthy. The tribe's contentment derived from
their peaceful co-existence with nature and themselves.

Because the people cared for one another, the elders who
made up the council were seldom given problems to arbi-
trate. They spent their combined wisdom settling minor
disputes between children. Furthermore, the tribe's medicine man predicted that the future of his people would
remain uncomplicated. The leadership of the chief was held
in the highest regard, for it was believed by all that he
possessed a special relationship with the Great Spirit which
continually ensured the tribe's good fortune. That was how
the people saw it, the elders accepted it, and the medicine
man explained it.

The chief of the Ndee was a gray-haired old man named
Shadow Bear. He was nearing sixty years of age and had
lived a good life. Having been chief for twenty years, he had
earned much honor and respect. Now, feeling that he would
soon join the spirits, he hoped to see his son, Painted Skin,
win the mantle of leadership. To accomplish this, his son
would have to be chosen by the council and tested by the
tribe's medicine man.

Black Wolf, the aging shaman of the tribe, had also
entered his waning years. Like the chief, he had earned a
position of great trust. Upon entering the twilight of his life,
he cherished one joy in particular. That joy was his daughter, Morning Shade. She was without question, the most
beautiful of the young women her age. She was full of life
and her heart was serene. Her spirit soared freely in the

warming days of summer. It soared because of the happiness she felt with her loving father and because of a great desire in her heart.

The center of Morning Shade's affection was a young brave in the prime of life. He was handsome, intelligent, strong of body and limb, and skilled in the arts of hunting and trapping. He was greatly admired by his fellow braves and respected by his father and his people. He, in turn, tried to earn their esteem by proving worthy of it. However, his greatest ambition in life was to marry Morning Shade, whom he had loved deeply since childhood. He was fully aware of the sacred custom that only a chief could marry the daughter of a medicine man. But that did not worry him, for he was Painted Skin, the son of Shadow Bear.

The rising sun in the sky splashed through the clouds, bathing the valley below. It gave everything the appearance of polished gold. The mountain winds blew playfully and the leaves danced. Yet despite the tranquility, there remained a noticeable absence of animal activity. The fresh valley air was accompanied by a melancholy silence.

There was inactivity in the glen, yet few paid attention to it. For the most part, people arose that morning with a sense of gladness. Their reason was apparent. This was the day Painted Skin and Morning Shade were to be wed. Their love was well-known and members of the tribe had encouraged them to become married. By noon, with the sun overhead, the people assembled to begin four days of celebration.

Everyone had planned for weeks for this occasion, especially the chief, who looked on proudly as his son donned a highly unusual black toga. In this beaded costume, the youth offered himself as a chief before the council and his people, to be accepted or rejected. If chosen, the young man would assume the leadership of the tribe when his father died. If not, other braves would challenge him for the honor.

As the tribe gathered, the drums began beating and the chief lit the bonfire. The wedding festival began. After many prayers were chanted, a special gift was offered to the Great Spirit. In this offering, the people asked for continued peace and happiness for the tribe. Then as the fire died down, the chief approached and placed a bundle in its flames. If the fire continued to burn clean, the request was granted by the

Father, who had approved the marriage. If not, dark _____ ve would indicate otherwise.

Accompanying the booming drums, the people sang proudly as the bundle burned in the flames. The chief turned away when the fire engulfed the special offering. For several minutes all was unchanged and the reddish glow remained clear. When at last, the medicine man appeared quite certain that the Great Spirit was pleased with the gift, he gave a knowing nod. The people then elevated the volume of their song.

However, just as the chanting reached its peak, the flames fell and a tiny thread of dark smoke began to appear at the center of the fire. The gathering stared in disbelief as the thread grew in size. Eventually, everyone stood stunned as a black column of smoke spiraled upward from the center of the camp. The medicine man turned pale, the chief was aghast, and the people, who had never witnessed a smoking ceremonial fire, became afraid.

"What can it mean, Black Wolf?" the chief asked.

"Is the Great Spirit displeased with us?" asked an elder.

"He must not desire the union of the two," said another.

"That cannot be true!" cried Morning Shade. "It cannot be!"

"I will demand the test of water," promised Painted Skin.

As the tribe's fears grew, a hundred voices went up from the crowd offering possible reasons for the omen. Then the medicine man, who had remained silent up until then, took his staff and held it aloft. Instantly the gathering took notice and became still. With all eyes on him, he walked to a mound where all could hear his words. He stood for a moment with a bowed head.

The hearts of the Ndee pounded in fear while the medicine man remained in thought. Across the land the sound of silence dwarfed everything. Finally, the medicine man raised his head to speak. Everyone drew near to listen.

"The sky was not darkened by the marriage, my people." There was pain in his strained voice. "Nor is it because the Great Spirit is displeased with us. It is not joy which darkens the sky, but rather unavoidable sadness."

"What sorrow do you speak of, Black Wolf?" questioned the chief. "Our people are happy. Our land is good, our lives are at peace. The children play happily. Our men are strong, our women sing gladly by the waters. The elders are not troubled. What then is this sorrow you speak of?"

"The sorrow of untold death which rises in the lands to the south." The medicine man explained carefully: "It lies many days journey from here, but I assure you it is coming toward us. They who come are an evil people, many times more cruel than anyone we can imagine. They swallow the fruits of the earth yet hunger for more. They are rich, but still they demand tribute. They do not accept life as a gift but rather as a token--a token they offer as a sacrifice to their God. Hear me well my people. I warn of a coming disaster, one in which our people must suffer greatly, one in which survival will be won or lost by one man's courage and one woman's love."

"He speaks of our children!" shouted Shadow Bear. "It is through them that our people will live or die! May their hearts be as strong as their love for the tasks ahead."

For ten days and nights, the Ndee dreaded the invasion from the south. While they waited, they deliberated on how to meet the threat. Some suggested that they offer the invaders their peace and friendship, while others counseled armed resistance. In the end, the former solution was reluctantly chosen. Against opposition, the wedding celebration too was postponed. On the tenth day, the southern menace arrived.

Fearing for the safety of their women and children, the Ndee hid them in the forest. There they stayed while the men assembled in the camp proper. The invaders did not seem overly concerned when they learned that they were expected. Their massive forces poured down into the valley, unrolling like a colossal hoard of army ants. The Ndee were awed by the thousands of brightly adorned headdresses which enhanced the feathered gold and silver garments of the strangers. Each warrior was armed with a bladed war club, spear, knife, and decorative shield.

At first, the Ndee counted five hundred invaders, then a thousand, then two thousand, until well over three thousand alien warriors swamped their camp, most of them wearing identical faces of death. The Ndee were alarmed, realizing their own lightly armed group numbered but five hundred. Each wondered what would happen next. They did not have to wait long, for the brightly-plumed leader of the invaders stepped forward and spoke:

"I am Queo-Tehi-Keu, warrior king of the Aztecs! Protected as I am by the golden powers of Quetzalcoatl, I have come for my tribute. There is no army in the world which can stop me from taking what is mine. I will not bargain for it. Since you expected me, you must know of our God and my power. Keep that in mind and we need waste few words."*

Shadow Bear, chief of the Ndee, was greatly impressed by the vast number of Aztecs, but still he could not find it in his heart to be afraid. Standing unarmed before the Aztec king, he spoke proudly and without fear.

"I am called Shadow Bear," he stated. "I am the voice of my people, who have lived in this valley since memory began. It is true, we were warned of your arrival. But we do not know of you, or your God, nor do we fear you. We do not pay tribute to anyone except the Giver of Life. We will gladly share what we have, but we offer it willingly. Accept it, and we can live in peace. If not, the wrath of our Father will avenge any harm you may inflict. I ask you to accept my gifts in friendship."

"They are not yours to offer old man!" screamed Queo-Tehi-Keu, "but mine to take. I will have all that I want and more! Much more! And because of your threat, I begin with your life."

The Aztec king gave a signal and a spear pierced Shadow Bear's chest. Upon seeing their chief murdered, the Ndee exploded in rage, like hornets whose nest has been ripped apart. In the densely packed camp, the three thousand Aztec warriors were unable to maneuver or use their strength, and they lost hundreds of men while dislodging themselves from the area. Once they attained the valley's

---

* Editor's note: As evident in these legends, the Apache had been exposed to Quetzalcoatl as an evil God, whereas to the Indians of ancient Mexico, he was a holy one who brought a religion of love. This religion later was corrupted. His counterpart, Tezcatlipoca, was considered the manifestation of darkness in human beings.

upper edge, they turned back upon the Ndee and, with precise fury, crushed the valiant and inexperienced Ndee tribe. In only hours, half of the Ndee warriors were killed and the rest were put in chains.

What happened next in the peaceful valley was so horrifying that few wished to recall it later. It began when the Aztecs located the women and children. Thereafter, the whole tribe was condemned to slavery and forced to build massive wood pyramids. What they were to be used for, the Ndee could only guess.

Once the giant pyramids were completed, the Aztec king ordered the wounded Ndee men taken to the altars at the top of the structures. There, one at a time, each victim was held tightly by four Aztec priests, while a fifth cut into the struggling man's chest and removed his heart. After all the victims had been sacrificed in this manner, they were left on the pyramid and it was set on fire.

For eight days, screams accompanied the Aztecs' bloody rituals. During those days, the Ndee prayed desperately to the Great Spirit, but the appalling scenes continued. Indeed, Queo-Tehi-Keu ordered even more fires. The Ndee could not understand their fate. And yet, unable to escape, they suffered as the pyramids continued to deplete their tribe. Having killed nearly all the adults, the Aztecs took two dozen screaming Ndee children and offered their lives to the Sun God. That was the most horrible day of all.

Pleading for mercy from their prison, the Ndee begged the Aztecs to spare the lives of their precious children, but to no avail. That night, the Great Spirit answered their prayers, and at last the ghastly rituals that had killed nearly all the captives were stopped. Queo-Tehi-Keu commanded his army to prepare the remaining prisoners for a journey to his capital city. There, he promised, the rest of them would die. But first, he would seek a final tribute.

The king of the Aztecs challenged any Ndee brave to step forward and willingly offer himself as a sacrifice. If he did, he would be granted any request, and he would be allowed to choose any woman for one day and a night. She would die with him.

Painted Skin was among the few survivors who missed being murdered during the days of slaughter. While the rest of the men shrunk from the thought of death, he un-hesitatingly volunteered. Morning Shade trembled at the horrid possibility that he would die alone. At the top of her voice, she begged to go with him. Curious as to why they would wish to die when so many had begged to live, the Aztec king ordered them brought before him. Immediately, he was struck by Morning Shade's beauty and asked if she wouldn't rather become his bride? She spat, stating she would prefer poison instead. Infuriated, Queo-Tehi-Keu ordered her "request" to be instant. But Painted Skin reminded the Aztec king to keep his word and give the girl to him. Reluctantly, he complied.

Painted Skin then raised a pledge to his people vowing he would not only die courageously, but would suffer death in complete silence. Doubting the young man's ability, the Aztec king laughed, prompting Painted Skin to challenge him to spare his remaining people if he succeeded. The Aztec ruler quickly agreed, adding that if he failed, Morning Shade should willingly become his slave. Painted Skin was about to decline, when Morning Shade confidently accepted the condition. Embracing each other closely, the two were led away.

A silent gloom stood guard over the tepee which housed Painted Skin and Morning Shade. They spent a restless night in each other's arms. Words of comfort and tears of happiness drifted softly between them as they lay reminisc-ing. Although offered food, neither ate. Instead, Painted Skin promised to Morning Shade his undying devotion, which he vowed would survive somehow. Morning Shade kissed him passionately and swore she too would always be near him.

The two condemned lovers spent their final hours thriftily. Neither one allowed a moment to slip away without reaffirm-ing their oath. Despite being exhausted, they could not sleep. Throughout the night they held each other close, listening to the slave builders construct the final funeral pyramid.

In the morning, the medicine man was allowed to visit them. The Great Spirit, the shaman informed them hastily, had appeared to him in a dream. In it, the Great Spirit had selected the young brave to destroy the invaders. Painted

Skin thanked him for the honor, but asked what one man could do against so many? Black Wolf did not elaborate; instead he advised the brave to wear his special black and gold beads which clung to his body like a second skin. Then he offered both prisoners a special mixture of herbs. Neither one hesitated to drink it. Thereafter, Black Wolf spoke solemnly:

"Painted Skin, son of Shadow Bear, you are now the Black Flame. Listen to my words. Accept the poison, for it shall become your weapon. Accept the flame, for it shall become your home. Accept the land, for it shall become your ally. Accept death, for men shall come to fear you. As your spirit fades, so will it dwell among us. Do not fear for your bride, the Sky Father promises that she shall be with you." Completing the ceremony, he led them before the Aztecs.

Standing magnificently adorned before their executioners, the youthful pair showed no fear. When the Aztecs produced the implements of death, a low frightful wail was heard among the spectators. Wearing a grin, the Aztec king sat on his throne seeking some trace of weakness in his victims. Finding none, he ordered the ordeal to begin.

Painted Skin was led up the tall pyramid, while his bride was encased in a beautifully crafted casket. Once secure, she too was carried aloft. Morning Shade closed her eyes and felt the poison relaxing her. She prayed that the Aztec king would keep his word to her people.

The Aztec priest was certain he could make the Ndee brave beg for mercy. Confidently, he encased the brave in a golden case which forced the victim to lie spread eagled. Then the priest slowly poured boiling oil into it. As it filled, the blistering liquid spilled from the arm and leg openings scalding several aids who screamed in agony. The victim remained quiet. Undaunted, the priest took an axe and, cutting through the soft metal, severed both of Painted Skin's hands. Blood gushed forth like a fountain, but no cry accompanied the cruelty.

The Aztecs were astonished by the Ndee's silence. The king suspected the brave had died instantly. But when the priest checked, Painted Skin smiled weakly. Enraged, the priest slammed the case shut and began hacking off limbs. First one foot, then the other, then one arm, then the second, and finally the priest ordered the golden case buried in flaming coals. Yet, no one heard a whimper from within the case.

When at last the priest conceded defeat, the scorched and mutilated body was dragged before the Aztec king. The medicine man came forward reminding him of his promise. Queo-Tehi-Keu, having no intention of honoring his word, ordered Painted Skin, who still lived, taken to the pyramid and sacrificed. In addition, he claimed the girl was his to do with as he wished. When it was learned she was dead, he furiously ordered her body burned as well.

Obeying the orders of their king, the Aztecs carried the two bodies to the top of the pyramid, then they set fire to the structure. With the Ndee looking on, the lovers were consumed within the inferno. The blaze became so intense that all observers were driven back by the heat. Eventually everything was incinerated. The Aztec king, convinced that the bodies were destroyed, ordered the remaining prisoners to be killed so no record of his treachery would exist. Armed with battle clubs, the warriors advanced on the Ndee who huddled together in their prison. Realizing they were about to die, they began chanting their death songs, thanking the Great Spirit for the good years he had bestowed on them. No one offered a single regret.

However, just as the Aztecs descended on the Ndee, the valley shook with a violent earthquake and broke with a shattering sound wave. Trees were flattened, mountains trembled, and all the people were petrified by a monstrous roar. Whatever it was, everyone, Aztecs and Ndee alike, searched for its origin. In their search they saw an image appearing in the center of the flaming pyramid, shimmering like polished diamonds. The Ndee marveled at the apparition, while the Aztecs cringed in fear. Quickly, they gathered around their terrified king.

Emerging from a volcanic womb, a gigantic reptile, glowing with the brilliance of hot coals, roared its arrival. Upon sighting the black and gold giant, the Aztecs scattered in panic. Those daring to gaze into the creature's blood-red eyes were instantly incinerated. While others, frozen with fear, were crushed by its massive body. Howling hysterically, the Aztec king ordered his warriors to attack the shimmering beast before it devoured him.

The Aztec warriors proved powerless and insignificant against the creature. The intense barrage of their spears, axes, and war clubs proved no match against its slashing ivory claws. With a cavernous mouth, the beast swallowed dozens of warriors at a time. After two thousand were killed, crushed or eaten, the rest scattered throughout the forest trying to find refuge.

The Aztec king sat paralyzed on his throne screaming in terror. Turning to the medicine man, he cried to know what it was. Proudly, the medicine man said, "Behold, the Black Flame is born." As the creature approached him, the Aztec fell to his knees, sobbing and begging for his life. He was promptly cleaved in two. The priests, attempting to escape the same fate, raced away in panic, plunging headlong into the cauldrons of boiling oil.

The Ndee, released from their prison by the fiery guardian, quickly traveled across the ravaged countryside. They could see the fleeing Aztecs in the distance. Meanwhile, the creature, having destroyed the invader, clawed its way up to the scenic mountain lake, while the Ndee made for the opposite crown of the valley.

After hours of exhausting effort, the Ndee climbed safely out of danger. Turning, they stared across the ashen plain below. Fires raged from the foothills to the summits. High atop the smoldering slopes, the reptilian creature which had emerged from the fire plunged into the boiling lake, bellowing its departure. Abruptly, everything became quiet. Then a horrendous explosion ripped the fabric of the molten mountain like tissue. The blast was followed by an earth wrenching quake and a tidal wave a hundred feet high, which forced the mountain to collapse inward into the fiery pit below.

The Ndee, watching from the mountain ridge, saw the colossal wave engulf the flaming valley. What used to be their home now lay under a hundred feet of water. For several days, the people mourned their dead. Then, following the surviving animals, they wandered away from the area, eventually becoming nomads.

Over the centuries, the Ndee occasionally return to their ancestral land. They do this to remember the departed spirits of that long-ago time. During the days of ceremony, visitors are sometimes permitted to observe the festive dances. This story may be one of those performed by the dancing story-tellers.

The land in which the legend took place can still be located. However, over the centuries it has changed dramatically. Today, the area is called the Gila wilderness. The people once called the Ndee are known as the Apache. Having learned what can come from being too peaceful, they became more aggressive fighters. Historians even suggest that they were the most feared of the Southwestern tribes when they were your enemy. The United States Army has described the Apache as "the finest light cavalry in the world."

Of the once beautiful valley, nothing remains except a vast wasteland where temperatures can soar over a hundred degrees, Fahrenheit. According to legend, the ancestral plain became known to the Ndee as the land of the Iron Tree. If one visits it, the reason for this designation is clear. The area is now a petrified forest. In this formidable landscape, one creature acts as its guardian and is easily recognized by its distinctive black and gold armor. The creature is the most poisonous lizard in the world. Embodying the spirit of Black Flame, it is generally known by its more familiar and perhaps more colorful title, the Gila Monster.

If you care to locate this formidable reptile, try looking for it near its favorite flower, which it seems to mysteriously prefer over all others. The golden colored shrub is known by some as the Morning Shade. One can only wonder if the spirit of Black Flame still embraces the spirit of his beloved.

Legend of the Twin Kings

(The Eagle and the Bear)

Long before the white man came and altered the traditional lives of the Native Americans, there was a race known as the "ancient ones," a spirit people credited with being the cultural wellspring of many Indian nations. From them came into being the knowledge which today survives as spirit songs. These songs are meant to teach the listener about courage and destiny, beauty and passion, and such qualities; they tell of the earthly guardians who were once men and women, and who later became the revered spirits of the earth. It is these spirits that we honor when we remember their songs.

This legend begins during the period of the migration of tribes entering the new continent. The wandering tribes were predominantly peaceful, but some thrived on warfare. Yet the hostility of these newcomers did not prevent the Ndee from acquiring an honored tradition of their own, known for its legendary exploits and for the courage and strength of its participants. To ensure that future generations would not forget the accomplishments of their ancestors, the storyteller learned to weave these tales skillfully and colorfully for the children. One such song spoke of two men destined to become the spirit fathers of new tribes.

Long ago, the Ndee lived in a thickly forested valley known as the Bright Leaf. In this green valley, Black Spear, the mighty leader of the people, was expecting his wife to soon give birth to a son. He was a tall, powerful, and fearsome warrior, who had been chosen to lead his braves in battle against marauding tribes. Because of his victories, his people assured him his firstborn son would succeed him as chief.

After a punishing winter, spring arrived again in the land of the Ndee. The sun and warm winds brought a new vitality to the valley and reassured its inhabitants. They had suffered greatly from both the harsh winter and the unfriendly tribes during the icy months. But they were a strong people. Their warriors were famed for their fierceness and courage. Their women were noted for their beauty, loyalty, and endurance. Aggressive tribes who foolishly attacked this combination of qualities soon discovered they were losing more than they were gaining. The enemy learned that tenacity was the trademark of the Ndee brave. He was not in the habit of yielding anything of value in battle, without forcing the attacker to pay dearly for it.

But in return for this fame, the Ndee paid a heavy price. Before the invaders arrived, they numbered some two thousand. Now, after a dozen years of hostilities, fewer than five hundred Ndee warriors remained. Still, their notoriety did allow some solace. Few marauding tribes, aware of the Ndee prowess, ever wished to challenge their reputation. Unfortunately, new migrating tribes, unaware of this distinction, were also accompanying the warm winds.

On account of the many Ndee adversaries, Black Spear became the binding tie of his people. Without him, the people would no doubt have lost their resolve and perished. Black Spear inspired heroics. In a bitter four-day winter battle, for example, which pitted two hundred Ndee warriors against an enemy five times their number, Black Spear risked every danger to encourage his men. They won, proving that Black Spear was their strength, but a strength which like the land, needed renewing.

It was midmorning in the seventh week of spring when scouts brought a warning of raiders approaching the Bright Leaf. The raiders were armed, painted, and appeared to be a large war party. While the women quickly gathered their children, the braves prepared to repulse the enemy. Despite the alarm of impending battle speeding through the camp, there was little outward sign of panic.

The tribe was orderly and calm as Black Spear walked through the camp. With a quiet demeanor, he stopped and stood in the camp's center, overseeing the preparations. A deep intensity was reflected in his dark face. He stood with his arms folded across his chest and his legs slightly apart. No trace of uncertainty showed in his eyes, which emitted a quiet power and were a source of inspiration to his tribe.

Black Spear mounted the horse prepared for him and turned to face his waiting warriors. The drums pounded as he studied their faces. Many were very young. He noted that few experienced warriors had survived the winter battles. He paused and reflected on their dwindling numbers. His heart saddened with the realization that more were destined to die. But what was the alternative? They had to defend their lives and land. His missing warriors had understood that, but it was of little comfort to the widows and mothers. This weighed heavily on Black Spear. But he did not fear death himself; instead, he was reassured by the knowledge that he and his wife were expecting a son destined to become a chief.

Black Spear and his warriors traveled a considerable distance from their camp before approaching the narrow entrance of a sandstone canyon. Before entering the rock-hewn passage, the chief sent scouts up the steep ridges to investigate the surroundings. They soon returned with news of the very discovery Black Spear had suspected.

From a captured raider, the scouts learned of a trap awaiting them just ahead. Furthermore, they discovered that a second raiding party had been sent by a roundabout way to attack the Ndee camp. Though concerned, Black Spear said nothing; instead he directed his braves to move stealthily up to the summit. At the top, he and his braves surprised the enemy below them and a battle took place. The enemy, pressing their superior numbers, hoped for an easy victory. Yet, after several hours, their numbers had gained them no advantage.

Meanwhile, far off in the Ndee camp, the alarm was given. The raider's second force was entering the camp. But because of Black Spear's foresight, the people were prepared. The raiders, thinking it would be an easy prize, rode boldly into the apparently deserted camp and were immediately cut down in mid-stride by a barrage of spears and arrows. The awaiting defenders charged from their many hiding places and engulfed the confused enemy. Despite being caught off guard, the raiders recaptured the advantage and within minutes were proving a threat to the defenders.

During the fierce contest, midwives were attending Black Spear's wife, who was delivering. Outside her tepee the battle raged, the agonized screams of dying people piercing the thin walls of the birthing tent. Soon the entire camp was on fire. A pallor of smoke hung over the valley. Human bodies and dead animals lay about like fragments of discarded cloth. Just as the expectant mother was enduring a contraction, the tepee was invaded by two raiders.

The Ndee midwives had suspected that Black Spear's wife might have her baby during the impending attack on their camp. As a precaution they had armed themselves. Thus, the instant the enemy broke into the tent, the courageous women sprang into action. In the confusion that followed, both the attackers and the midwives were killed, and the tent came crashing down.

Black Spear's wife lay smothered beneath the remnants of her tepee. She was not concerned about being discovered, nor bothered by the threat of encroaching fires. She was mindful of only one thing, giving birth. Her head throbbed like an angry tom-tom, aggravated by the violent sounds just outside her tent. The painful swelling inside her womb commanded her immediate attention. During her final labors she screamed twice, then she fainted.

When at last the Ndee had routed the invaders, the women who were not busy caring for the wounded went to aid the chief's wife. Coming to her tepee, they released her from the tangle of poles, bodies, and hides. To their surprise, they discovered she had delivered not one but two baby boys. This made everyone happy. Even in the midst of war, new life had come. A great cheer went up from the defenders of the camp as they praised the wife of the chief for giving him two heirs.

However, the excitement died in the dawning realization that only the firstborn was promised the privilege of being their next chief. As the crowd looked upon the two infants, they puzzled over the problem of which child had been born first. No one, not even the mother, knew. They could only hope Black Spear would live to sort it out.

It took days for the Ndee tribe to recover from the raid. But their recovery was strengthened when they learned the enemy had lost nearly all of its forces during the battle or in retreating from it. Their pride redoubled when Black Spear and his warriors returned. They had not only defeated the enemy, but had accepted their offer of peace. "They are clansmen from the Snake River," Black Spear told his people, "and I have accepted their bond as repayment for the injury inflicted." Since the Ndee were not vindictive, they accepted the raider's pledge. In addition, they allowed them a portion of land along the river. Thereafter, their neighbors lived in peace with them.

Black Spear and his people decided to celebrate their victory. During the ceremony, happiness over the newborn twins dominated the festive air. Pride for the chief, his warriors, and their triumphs filled their songs. Many weeks after the battle, the celebration continued.

Months later, however, the question of the chief's two sons was still unresolved. The council deliberated endlessly on the problem and it was beginning to create uncertainty. While the council debated, Black Spear fulfilled a tribal tradition for his newborn sons. During a nighttime bonfire, the chief presented the medicine man with a gift, and then brought his infant sons before the assembled tribe. Holding each aloft in turn, he asked that their names be spoken and accepted as part of the Ndee Brotherhood. After a solemn chant, the wise one asked Black Spear to say the names aloud. "This boy will be called Bright Cloud!" said the father proudly. "And this, my other son, will be known as Iron Claw." The medicine man then repeated the names and prophesied that the boys would become invincible in manhood.

Following the raider battle, the Ndee tribe enjoyed twenty years of peace. The long peace and an abundance of game and good weather allowed them to prosper. However, the perplexing problem of the twins remained unresolved. By now, there was considerable concern over the succession of leadership. Since both youths were proving remarkable, their admirers were divided.

The tribe had grown to nearly two thousand braves once again. Among their ranks, Bright Cloud surpassed all others

in the use of the bow, spear, and war axe. He was also
nicknamed Swift One because of his extraordinary skills in
running, climbing, and stealth. His ability in tracking was
equally admired. The council was impressed with the young
brave.

There was only one man who could match the feats of
Bright Cloud. He was Iron Claw, Bright Cloud's twin
brother. In brute power, tenacity, and valor, Iron Claw
towered over everyone. He could not shoot a bow as well as
Bright Cloud, but neither could Bright Cloud lift a canoe full
of warriors out of the river as he could. Iron Claw could not
throw a spear as accurately as his brother, but when he
hurled it, its distance could not be equaled. Though Bright
Cloud could best others in the use of the war axe, he was
hard pressed to beat his brother in open hand combat.
During their matches, Bright Cloud was acclaimed a worthy
opponent, but Iron Claw always won. In nearly every contest, Bright Cloud proved more agile, and Iron Claw consis-
tently stronger. The elders agreed, as a hunter, Bright Cloud
was artistic, but Iron Claw was just as successful. It was a
difficult choice between the two. Half the council wanted
Bright Cloud to be the next chief, while the other half chose
Iron Claw. The people were similarly polarized.

The passage of twenty years had added new wrinkles to
the troubled brow of Black Spear. His people were becoming
increasingly undecided as to which son should follow him.
The warriors demanded that one son be chosen soon, and
to this end they made their voices heard at the council fire.
The women felt the confusion too. Their children were
constantly bickering over which was the superior twin.

As the tribe grew impatient, the council began pressing
the chief to select one son, since the tribe itself was dead-
locked on the issue. Black Spear felt the burden settling
upon his aging shoulders. He had to decide. But how? His
heart was divided too. Aside from their dissimilar achievements, both his sons were equally qualified to assume the
burden of leadership. In addition, he loved them equally
with an overwhelming pride. Still, the tribe was right. He
was feeling tired. If only there was some way he could
decide. It did no good to ask his people. They were equal in

numbers for both sons. If he asked his sons, both openly desired to succeed him. Each felt destiny awaited him.

Finally, the medicine man advised Black Spear to take his problem up to the summit of the Spirit Mountain. For several days, Black Spear fasted and prayed on the mountain to the Giver of Life. He informed the Great Spirit of his need and appealed for his help. Regardless of his choice, he admitted, one of his sons and half of his people would be disappointed. The thunder of the mountain became the voice of the Great Spirit. It informed Black Spear that his problem was understood. The Great Spirit knew which son was born first. This made the old chief happy. At last, he would learn which son was his rightful heir. Yet, when he asked, the voice only responded by requesting the presence of his twins sons.

On returning to the camp, Black Spear found his people troubled. The council informed him of the events which had happened during his absence. Two days ago, they said, a marauding tribe had attacked their ally, the Snake River people. As the raiders were expected to return, the Snake River people had come and asked the Ndee warriors for help.

Unhesitatingly, Black Spear's sons had taken volunteer warriors to aid their friends. However, they had left a sufficient number of warriors behind to protect the Ndee camp. On hearing this news, Black Spear took additional braves as reinforcements and journeyed to the site of the conflict. On arrival at the Snake River camp, Black Spear discovered that the conflict had been brief. With the help of the Ndee, the Snake River warriors had defeated the invaders.

From the Snake River chief, Black Spear learned of the furious three-day battle in which both Bright Cloud and Iron Claw had been killed. The Snake River women, who greatly admired the sons, expressed their sorrow to Black Spear by ceremoniously cutting off the smallest finger of their left hands. The Snake River chief expressed his gratitude to Black Spear by assuring him that his sons' names would live forever in the honored songs of his people.

Much later, at the Ndee camp, the Snake River chief related to everyone how courageously Black Spear's sons had fought. He described in great detail how Bright Cloud and his braves had chased the enemy into the mountains.

There, within the confines of a narrow canyon, a desperate conflict took place. During the din of battle, it was Bright Cloud's earsplitting war cry which inspired bravery in those who fought at his side. Then a strange thing happened. After the battle, Bright Cloud was nowhere to be found, not even among the dead.

Meanwhile, Iron Claw had engaged a large segment of raiders in the dense forest east of the Snake River tribe camp. He was last seen surrounded by the encroaching enemy, swinging a battle club and roaring a war cry which echoed through the forest like a raging storm. The enemy had never witnessed such fury in any warrior. But, despite Iron Claw's great strength and courage, the situation became hopeless in the face of overwhelming odds.

Even as Iron Claw's dwindling group was slowly engulfed, they fought on with such tenacity, it made the Snake River warriors proud to be among the Ndee braves. Hours later, after the battle, a shroud of silence fell over the dark forest. When reinforcements arrived, they searched for the valiant leader. But despite much effort, the searchers were unable to locate Iron Claw.

The next day, Black Spear spent hours diligently searching for the bodies of his sons. Finally, admitting failure, he and his warriors returned home and performed a death ritual for those lost in battle. The ceremony lasted for several days. Afterwards, the chief returned to the Spirit Mountain. There he would explain to the Great Spirit why his sons were unable to join him.

As he climbed, Black Spear felt his age. Still, he resolutely trudged up the side of the rugged, tree-covered mountain. A heavy snow began falling, and a chilling wind numbed his hands and feet. Disregarding the discomfort, Black Spear forced himself upward. The arduous effort exhausted the old man. Adding to his weakness was the fact that he had not eaten in days. Now, the combination of fatigue and hunger forced him to surrender to the wintry elements.

Exhausted, Black Spear fell heavily into the soft carpet of snow, realizing he would soon join his sons. He was certain he could not continue without nourishment, but he did not have the strength to hunt. Reluctantly, he resigned himself to staring into an icy river which was slowly being enshrouded by snow.

Much later, he turned slowly onto his back, seeking comfort in his death bed. Black Spear thought about death and was not afraid. He had had a good life. His only regret was that he had lost his sons without seeing them become the legendary fathers the medicine man had prophesied. They could have achieved so much, he thought. His eyes roamed across the dismal sky, and he felt sleepy. Suddenly, he spied a large solitary bird flying high above him as though it was searching for something.

For long, frigid minutes, Black Spear lay motionless, admiring the grace and ease of the lofty form. As he followed it with his eyes, the powerful apparition suddenly plummeted downward in an unexpected burst of speed, then careened sharply across the river. Without any noticeable effort, its great claws pinched the waters and snatched up a large fish. With the catch firmly held, the bird flew again into the overcast sky. Moments later, it swung low, and passing directly over the astonished Black Spear, dropped the prize into his lap. Then with an ear-piercing scream, the great bird disappeared among the clouds.

After eating the fish and satisfying his hunger, Black Spear resumed his trip to the mountain summit. The bird was magnificent, he thought. It was unlike any he had ever seen. Its plumage was golden brown with a beautiful crown of white feathers. Distracted by thoughts of the bird's image, Black Spear suddenly discovered he had inadvertently strayed into a large circle of waiting timber wolves.

As the wolves arranged themselves in a phalanx of sharp white teeth, Black Spear slowly drew his knife and prepared to battle the deadly pack. At that instant, the snowy earth shook violently, and a towering, massive animal charged into the tightening circle of starving wolves. The shaggy, brown beast tore viciously at the savage band, and within seconds had killed ten wolves and injured eight others. The remaining wolves scattered into the thickets, yelping their surrender. Black Spear stood frozen to the spot, unable to fathom what had taken place.

After the last wolf disappeared, the lumbering giant turned to face Black Spear, rising to its full height of eight feet. Unexpectedly, the creature held up a bloodied right paw and waited. Awed by the bizarre event, Black Spear mechanically raised his own arm and opened his hand. Leisurely, the beast lowered itself, then turned about and disappeared into the woods, leaving Black Spear completely puzzled.

"Your sons have each become the fathers of a new race," thundered the Great Spirit. "Bright Cloud is now the king of the air. It was he who fed you at the river's edge. Iron Claw saved your life from the wolves and will be known as the forest king. Forever they will inspire the lives of men. Go now and tell your people. You will yet live to guide them for twenty more years. After that time, your sons will return to help your people select a new chief."

Today, among the Apache and the descendants of the Snake River people, often referred to as the Comanche, are those who recall their spirit forefathers in a ritual song, sung during the inauguration of a new chief. In these tribes, the eagle and the bear are believed to be their spirit ancestors.

Legend of the Desert Guardian

(The Rattlesnake)

Softly mighty desert
Choose the gentle stride.
Heed the Desert Guardian
or choose a place to die.

In the Rocky Mountains of the American Southwest can be found some interesting and dangerous interior passageways. Some are the only means of passage between one mountain valley and another. These corridors are all aptly named. Santo's Canyon, for instance, is located in the nearly impregnable Superstition Mountains of Arizona. This narrow pass is neatly wedged between walls of stone that soar hundreds of feet high. During the Spanish Exploration, this strategic point was held for ten days by retreating conquistadors against an army of avenging natives. The grateful Spaniards, having survived the onslaught, christened the pass after their patron saints.

Another mountain corridor is Pasa Suerte, a high alpine opening with narrow shoulders and a horrendously curved spinal gap. Situated two hundred miles inland along the Baja Peninsula, it was once known as the Lucky Pass. Lucky, because those who survived it were fortunate. However, the most notorious desert passageway in the American Southwest, and the origin of this Apache legend, is known as La Culebra pass, or the Snake Pass; also known as El Paso (the Pass). In ancient times, this corridor, embedded now between the border of two modern countries, was called the Devil's Throat. South of this desert gateway lay the arid wastelands of the Sierra Diablo, while north of it lived the nomadic Apache who called themselves"Children of the Wind." This is their story of the Desert Guardian.

The Apache were a kind and simple people. Their modest goal in life was to fulfill a destiny promised them by the Great Spirit. Someday, the promise revealed, one member of the tribe would make them invincible and immortal. Everyone naturally expected the chief to be that man, but even though many chiefs had come and gone, none had ever fulfilled the prophecy. Still, the believers never lost hope. Among the people was a quiet old man who had never sought to attract attention to himself. He studied the magic of plants, contrived potions, and knew the power of songs. He was by far the oldest member of the community, having reached seventy years of age. The people knew that the older a man was, the wiser he was deemed to be, and thus deserving of greater respect. As a result, the oldest, wisest, and most respected individual in the tribe was Mo-Kesh, meaning golden eyes. He was the first medicine man.

The homeland of Mo-Kesh and his tribe was located on a broad range of green-covered earth which extended twenty miles in radius. Despite its nearly flat appearance, it was in the beveled curve of a river valley. Rising and falling with regularity were long stretches of grasslands, beaver ponds, and brown hills which, when viewed from aloft, completely surrounded the Apache camp. Hemming the eastward side of the camp was a fast flowing river bulwarked by acres of marshlands. West of the camp rose miles of encircling snowcapped mountains. From base to summit, they loomed over the expanse like sentinels. Year-round, the forested slopes not only provided the icy waters which flowed across the broad valley, but also an abundance of game.

To the north of the valley lay vast virgin territories, encompassing several thousand miles of open land, which nuzzled lazily against the blue horizon. The tribe, aware of these lands, rarely desired them. They were perfectly content to remain where they were. Although not enticed by the north, they were apprehensive concerning the south, where one protective mountain lay between them and the desert on its south. The southern face of this mountain was nearly impossible to climb and treacherous in every respect.

Though many murderous trails were etched on its face, none led anywhere.

Though unscalable, the mountain was not completely impregnable. It did contain one secret passageway through the middle of its fortresslike walls. The tribe, aware of the danger of traveling this mountain, did not often venture beyond it. It was rumored that far beyond the pass, deep within the southern desert, lived a brutal race of people who practiced ritual blood sacrifice, ate human flesh, and worshiped the golden image of a feathered serpent. This knowledge made the peace-loving Apache apprehensive, lest sometime their ferocious neighbors would learn of their peaceful existence and be tempted to send an expedition against them.

This Apache tribe numbered five hundred people. Foremost among them, and dominating a circle of well known figures, was Iron Lance. For a hunter, that was a proud name. He had recently been chosen to lead the tribe for he was recognized as a brave and skilled warrior. Tall and handsome, his youthful face reflected courage. Many openly admired his choice of Gentle Rain to be his wife.

Together their moods became a measure of the tranquility of the tribe. When they were happy, so too were the people. When they suffered a loss or sorrow, the tribe bore their grief. Yet, all things considered, life generally went well for everyone, and the chief spared no effort to maintain a sense of contentment. If there was a conflict between members of the tribe, the chief settled the matter quickly and auspiciously to everyone's satisfaction. Thus tribal tensions were kept to a minimum.

One day, while the people were busy preparing for a celebration, a stranger was seen coming through the pass of the mountain. Since no one could enter the passage without being spotted, he was easily followed along the trail. As the man raced quickly along the dirt path, he glanced fearfully backward, as though running from something. His soft white tunic, beautifully embroidered with gold and silver figures, glittered like polished glass, as did his gold tiara and rich jewelry. His shiny black hair was laced with solid gold pins and jeweled broaches. As the man ran, his silver knee-length sandals left light impressions on the floor of the pass. At last, completely exhausted, the stranger arrived at the center of the camp, where he begged for safety and water.

In the space of a few minutes, the majority of the tribe assembled in the middle of the camp. As the people arrived, they speculated on the stranger's identity, creating a drone which eventually brought the chief and his wife to the scene. They too studied the intriguing stranger, who lay resting on the ground. Gentle Rain knelt beside him, offering a pitcher of water. The man snatched it with both hands and drank quickly and greedily. As he drank, there was a gasp among the spectators, who were not stunned by his thirst but by the lacerations and rope burns on his wrists. More groans of pity were added when they noticed other wounds on his body.

The people surmised that the stranger had recently escaped from some torturous treatment. The chief, eying the man closely, concluded he was not from any of the northern tribes. The stranger's face was tan and well defined. He had green eyes, high cheekbones, and a well-groomed head. His thirst quenched, the stranger allowed the jug to drop next to Gentle Rain. The chief knelt beside her and reached to examine a jeweled medallion about the man's neck. The stranger did not protest. Indeed, when he realized the chief's intent, he smiled and offered the necklace to him. As the chief took it, the stranger fainted.

While some of the women attended the injured man, the chief stood inspecting the necklace. Minutes later, the women informed him that the stranger was near death. The chief implored them to save him, but the women shrugged, saying that only Mo-Kesh might be able to save the stranger. The chief knew of Mo-Kesh and his dark potions, herbs, and chants, but he wondered if the stranger wouldn't tax his magical powers.

When Mo-Kesh approached, Iron Lance studied him intently. Mo-Kesh was a gray-haired old man whose deeply wrinkled, weatherbeaten face unintentionally masked whatever emotion lay behind it. The curious thing about him was his yellow eyes. Up close, they seemed glassy and glazed, and made people nervous during conversations. The chief observed with pity the man's torn shirt, patched trousers, and ragged moccasins. This tattered combination had become identified as belonging to no one else. Still, despite his aging bone vest and crooked staff, he was highly respected. However, he remained quite mysterious. As Mo-Kesh ambled through the parting crowd the chief met him and smiled, but if the old man smiled back, he could not tell. Nevertheless, he pointed to the injured man, asking Mo-Kesh if he could save him.

"I must know where he comes from, Mo-Kesh!" implored the chief.

"I will do what I can," replied Mo-Kesh in a whisper which sounded more like a hiss. "This man isn't dead, but he should be. It may be too late."

"We entrust him to you, Mo-Kesh," finished the chief, as he turned to show the medallion to the people. While the chief spoke, Mo-Kesh opened his medicine pouch, and, in a series of curious motions, prepared and administered various potions to the stranger. Later, Mo-Kesh began chanting quietly. The unconscious man remained completely lifeless."

"Is he dead?" questioned the chief, disappointed.

"No, Iron Lance," answered Mo-Kesh. "He is not dead, but he must sleep now. In time you may question him." The old man stood and uncoiled himself with some difficulty, then departed. Thereafter Iron Lance ordered the stranger taken away to a place of rest, while the crowd dispersed.

Several days later, the stranger awoke and found Mo-Kesh's yellow eyes glaring down at him. The stranger instantly recoiled from the hypnotic stare and then his surprise turned to embarrassment as he noticed others were present. Sitting in a semi-circle near the edges of a great tepee were Mo-Kesh, Iron Lance, and Gentle Rain. They all sat some distance across from him. When she saw him awaken, Gentle Rain arose and offered food to him. The stranger was hesitant until he recognized her face.

Throughout the morning, the stranger spoke freely, giving his name as Quir-Ri-Gua, meaning Bright Spirit. He explained that he was from a tribe a thousand miles to the south of the pass. He spoke unrestrainedly until they asked about his wounds. Instantly, he was silent and his face paled. Only after repeated assurances that he was among friends did Quir-Ri-Gua begin speaking again. The young man tearfully revealed that he was the last survivor of a once proud nation.

He told a long and painful story of how his people had been murdered systematically by savages living in a city built on a lake. Unlike the rest of his unfortunate clan, he had been selected and allowed one year to live. During that time, he was crowned a sun king and granted his every whim. Regardless of what he desired, from gold to exotic pleasures, nothing was withheld. For twelve glorious months he lived in absolute splendor. However, once the year was over, he discovered the ghastly fate awaiting all sun kings. They were sacrificed like fatted calves, cooked, and then eaten by worshipers of a Feathered Serpent. Quir-Ri-Gua had miraculously managed to escape in the midst of being prepared for this special human sacrifice. This story petrified his listeners, including those standing just outside the tepee. The people immediately considered the dangers of harboring an escaped sun king.

While the people pondered their fate, loyalties became strained over whether Quir-Ri-Gua should be allowed to remain in the camp or sent away. Many worries were echoed in the council. The warriors of the tribe, although in sympathy with the council and having voiced concern for their families, nevertheless stated that they would obey the decisions of the chief.

However, during those troubling days, the chief himself was at odds. Night after night he pondered the problem. On the one hand, he could return Quir-Ri-Gua to his captors and perhaps avert a war, but that would mean being party to human sacrifice. Alternatively, he could shelter him, in which case he would be endangering all his people. Iron Lance thought the problem hopeless, and sought the advice of Mo-Kesh. The wise man urged the chief to consider what might happen if the savages were not content with one victim? Might they not want those who helped the prisoner for their next sacrifices? Convinced by the old man's wisdom, Iron Lance advised his troubled people that their guest would stay. He reminded everyone that Quir-Ri-Gua's life had been entrusted to them by the Great Spirit. It was up to the tribe to be worthy of it. The chief asked his people to wait patiently.

What the chief was waiting for did not take long to arrive. Exactly eight days after Quir-Ri-Gua's arrival, more strangers were spotted in the pass. This group of men marched arrogantly, pridefully, and without fear, as though the pass belonged to them. The lookouts counted twenty men in bright, colorful array, and hurriedly reported the news to the chief. Without the least bit of apprehension, caution, or concern, the newcomers marched defiantly through the pass and straight into the middle of the Apache camp.

The strangers who stood before the Apache were a magnificent sight. Yet, one look at their menacing features told them that Quir-Ri-Qua was not one of them. Their cruel expressions revolted the people. But if the strangers cared, they did not show it. Indeed, they stood proud, aloof, and silent.

The Apache gathered, slowly forming a circle around the elegantly painted visitors. Then Iron Lance arrived with his wife, both wearing their ceremonial splendor. As the chief took his place at the head of the circle, latecomers hurried and jostled for last minute positions. Sitting down, Iron Lance studied the strange warriors closely.

They were not a tall people, he observed; hardly any were even of average height. Though small in stature, they were nonetheless muscular. Their stocky arms and legs indicated that they might be craftsmen, forgers, or miners. These occupations would explain their golden armor and excessive jewelry which encrusted their majestic battle gear. The gorgeous costumes were a distracting, dazzling display.

For several minutes the gaudy strangers stood silently, inviting the gawking spectators' appreciation. The crowd buzzed with apprehension as they observed that the strangers were armed with richly adorned shields, axes, spears, and machetes. Iron Lance scrutinized their dark faces, each decorated with bright flashes of paint. Their fierce expressions were framed with feathered war bonnets of lengthy multicolored plumes. Their embroidered white tunics, embellished with gold and black threads, duplicated Quir-Ri-Gua's apparel of the day he had appeared, half dead, in their camp.

Black clouds drifted overhead casting a gray gloom on the tense assemblage below in the Apache Camp. One cloud of immense proportions shadowed the face of the most vicious looking stranger, cuing a response. Handing his shield to his aid, the formidable warrior took several steps forward and stood boldly before Iron Lance's chair.

"I am Tepetatte!" he shouted, endeavoring to reach everyone within earshot, "brother to Lord Xochimilco, king of the Zapotecs! It is his voice I bring to you! Listen well, valley people; heed my brother's words! If you do not, you will surely come to regret this day!"

"I am Iron Lance, chief of the Apache!" Iron Lance replied proudly. "I am the ears of my people! Speak your brother's words."

"Heed well, Iron Lance," Tepetatte warned, strutting proudly. "You are known to be harboring a man called Quir-Ri-Qua! He is ours by law and we demand you deliver him! Failure to obey will bring dishonor to our God and ultimate destruction to your people! I demand that you bring him to us at once!"

"And if not!" responded Iron Lance curiously and without fear.

"We shall take him!" promised Tepetatte, lifting his spear.

"Tepetatte, brother of Xochimilco, listen to my answer!" the chief replied, standing up. "It is true Quir-Ri-Qua is here. But we cannot release him to your law. He has told us of your God and your barbaric practices! We cannot, in all that is honorable, fulfill your demand. Tell your brother we do not wish to dishonor your God with a war, but we believe that by giving him to you we would dishonor our own Sky Father. Therefore, I will allow you to take only your lives. Choose to return and I will not guarantee them again."

Upon hearing Iron Lance's reply, the Zapotecs flared angrily, making a feint at attacking him. However, when they saw five hundred spears raised in his defense, they froze. Tepetatte and his men, realizing the hopelessness of the situation, backed away. Cursing the chief and his people, Tepetatte and his warriors turned wrathfully and left the camp, vowing to return.

Once they had gone, the whole camp exploded with concern over their fate. Many argued aloud about how long it would take the army of the Zapotecs to return. When Quir-Ri-Gua appeared, he suggested he be allowed to surrender himself, since the strength of the enemy was well over ten thousand. His humble suggestion was rejected with the reminder that the chief had given his word.

"What shall we do, then?" asked the more fearful in the crowd.

"They are massing even now!" warned two lookouts racing into camp, exhausted. "We saw them clearly marching toward us about ten miles away!"

"We shall leave a small force to cover our escape," advised the chief. "Then we shall take our families and go north. There they cannot find us."

"Escape?!" questioned voices in the crowd. "Why should we give up our homes for a stranger? Why should we have to leave our land?"

"There is a time to fight!" explained the chief. "But we shall select the time and place. For now, that decision rests with the Great Spirit." With the majority of the people agreeing, Mo-Kesh, the old man, suddenly and quite mysteriously appeared among them. "I will go into the pass and hold the savages," he promised. "I will go alone. Depart if you must, or stay if you will. But I assure you, the enemy will not follow, because I will remain and guard the land for you."

The tribe was amused by the ridiculous proposal of Mo-Kesh. It was preposterous to think that one man considered himself the equal of an army. But the laughter died when they realized the old man was serious. One look into his yellow eyes and even the chief was convinced. When asked if he desired a change of battle clothes, Mo-Kesh informed the chief that the Great Spirit had promised him one. He added that hereafter, the Ndee would run from no enemy. Gentle Rain pleaded with him to reconsider the danger.

"Do not fear for me," Mo-Kesh stated confidently. "I shall never leave my people unprotected. I am told by the Great Spirit that our tribe will become immortal and invincible if I succeed. So I must try." The tribe watched as the chief reluctantly agreed to rely on Mo-Kesh and his magic. As the revered and respected old man walked away from the camp, the women began weeping.

An hour later, the Apache were informed that the army of the Zapotecs were entering the pass. Much to the astonishment of all, the chief ordered everyone to sit and wait. There were some in the camp who thought this insane and decided to disobey. But when the few saw the majority staying, they put away their fear and joined them in the center of the camp. Once there, they began drumming a beat and reciting a long prayerful chant.

Meanwhile, the Zapotecs had reached the midpoint of the mountain pass where they found that the sole means of defense offered by the Apache was a raggedy old man, menacing them with a painted gourd and a long stick tipped with two needles. A great roar of laughter echoed off the stone walls when they saw and heard the old man chanting and dancing in a circle. Tepetatte was indignant. He ordered the old man killed quickly so that they might get on with the serious business.

"Stand your ground, savages!" ordered Mo-Kesh, sprinkling the road with tiny colored granules. "Come closer and you will never see home again!" Raucous laughter, sneers, and rude imitations followed Mo-Kesh's warning. Soon, however, the old man's yellow eyes began to radiate eerily, and a low hissing sound, rising in volume, caught his enemy's fixed attention, rendering them speechless.

The marching warriors heard it and quickly froze in their tracks, afraid to move. A new sound, like the one made by a vibrating tambourine, was clearly a warning to stay back. It originated within the tiny rattle Mo-Kesh was shaking lightly in his hand. Tepetatte noticed his other hand held the flexing rod which featured two lengthy needles. The thin tips glowed brightly like two white hot branding irons. As their mysterious adversary danced in his sand-painted circle, the warriors closed in further. Mo-Kesh was aware of them but remained unconcerned, increasing his hissing, causing the golden-plumed warriors to hesitate. However, Tepetatte goaded, chided, and ridiculed his men into advancing on the single, chanting Apache.

Arriving within ten feet of Mo-Kesh, they raised their weapons, while the rattle grew louder and louder. When they reached the old man, he suddenly disappeared in a puff of black smoke which enveloped the pass. Instantly, the rattling ceased and cries of pain exploded from the warriors. In the dimness, Tepetatte saw a large number of his elite warriors falling to the ground, gripping their arms, legs, hands, and necks, screaming as if they were being burned alive. Frustrated, angry, and impatient, he grabbed a spear and charged forward blindly himself.

What transpired next Tepetatte found impossible to believe. Attacking what should have been the old man, he came instead face to face with a towering set of glowing, yellow eyes, inset within the head of a gigantic snake. Abandoning his courage, he dropped his spear and shield, and turned to run. However, before he could act, the eyes hypnotized him in place, while huge fangs struck his body. Instantly, he felt a blue fire surging through his veins. In his agony, Tepetatte forgot his purpose and went crashing headlong into the spears of his advancing troops in a mad dash to escape the pain.

With the fog shrouding the pass, the lookouts above were unable to see anything below. Despite this, they were able to hear the echoing wails of tortured men. Down in the pass, other unsuspecting soldiers struggled over the dead to reach the same end. The remaining warriors recoiled, trampling the unlucky underfoot in their frenzied haste to retreat.

Several hours later, Iron Lance and his men entered the pass to discover what had taken place. What they discovered was incredible! Carpeting the entire pass, lay the bodies of a thousand dead warriors. Lookouts, tracing the retreating enemy, informed the chief that the remainder had disappeared.

"So what has become of Mo-Kesh?" Iron Lance wondered. Unable to find Mo-Kesh or his body, he ordered the pass cleared. As his men began carrying corpses away, Iron Lance noticed two small red puncture marks on each victim.

"Could this have been the cause of death?" he speculated thoughtfully. "If so, what was the source?" By late evening, nothing was found of the medicine man, so Iron Lance discontinued the search and instructed the tribe to prepare a ceremonial funeral for Mo-Kesh.

It was much later when Gentle Rain questioned her husband concerning the mysterious incident. Iron Lance described how he had found the enemy, but no trace of Mo-Kesh. The old man had disappeared. Quir-Ri-Gua had vanished too, she said. No one in the camp could find a trace of him. Troubling as the disappearances were, the chief believed their spirits would in good time reveal themselves.

Months later, the search all but forgotten, Iron Lance and his men found themselves in the mountain pass. Nearing its southern entrance, they came upon a curious sound which imitated a gently vibrating tambourine. The sound caused them to freeze instantly. Advising no movement, Iron Lance took several cautious steps forward, searching for the source.

Nearing two boulders, he found what he was seeking. Signaling his men to advance slowly, Iron Lance pointed to a huge snake coiled strategically near the mouth of the pass. The group watched in awe as the massive reptile nervously coiled itself into a tighter circle. Like an ominous banner, its rattling tail was held aloft, while its yellow eyes stared back at them hypnotically. Admiring the wondrous creature, the men surmised it would be a force to be feared. There was a strange, compelling magic about it.

Although the rattling became intense and the snake's eerie eyes glowed, Iron Lance moved closer studying the snake's unusual skin patterns. They were large, quilted, gray-brown patches, resembling diamonds. The scaly skin surface had a newness, yet long pieces of dead skin hung loosely from it. Suddenly, the chief smiled knowingly. Stepping away he said, "So, Mo-Kesh, the Great Spirit did give you some new clothes and a great new power. Take care old friend, we shall always remember you."

Centuries have passed since the legend of Mo-Kesh was first recited. But his prophecies did come true. The Apache, as a fighting force, have never been afraid of an enemy, nor have they ever been officially beaten in battle. Despite betrayal by some of their own people who served as scouts and helped track the most famous Apache chieftains, the Apache warrior remained invincible. Their hunting, tracking, and fighting abilities are legendary and have made them immortal. The United States Army's lack of success against them caused one general to declare: "Fighting the Apache is like fighting the wind." Thus they earned their name, the Children of the Wind.

As for the mysterious stranger, it is believed that he was the Great Spirit testing the tribe's beliefs. His supposed orig-

inal homeland came to be known as the Land of the Vanished Spirit. Today, New Mexicans call it White Sands.

As for Mo-Kesh, the first medicine man, he has become the symbol of mystery and death. People who seek him are well aware of his poisonous bite. If you are daring enough to look for Mo-Kesh, remember, he will warn you only once. His warning is the most distinctive sound in the world. Once you hear it, you will know you are near the American diamond-back rattlesnake. Of course, the Apache just prefer to remember him as the Desert Guardian.

Legend of the Wind Dancer

(The Hummingbird)

Centuries ago, the ancestors of the Apache lived in the open expanse of America which would one day be called the Great Plains. These people were warrior nomads who later took root in the heart of the Southwest. Once established, their children were schooled in their origins by the old ones in the tribe. It was they who recalled the stories of events long past and who taught the songs which became tribal legends such as the following.

In the middle of the Great Plains was an area known as the Trembling Earth. It acquired its name from the seasonal return of vast herds of buffalo to the central plain. Here, too, lived the Ndee, in a valley alongside a winding river. The seasons of the year were known to the Ndee, and were measured by members of the tribe who noted the movements of the sun and the waxing and waning of the moon. Their yearly observations were begun by giving the month in which the buffalo returned the name of a spirit animal. This name was selected by the tribal medicine man. It was he who, after reading the spirit signs and natural omens, christened the new year.

Because of the longevity and severity of the winter, during which half the tribe nearly died, and because the only animal observed on the white, winter expanse of the plain was a furry, ebony fox, the medicine man augured ill, calling the year in question the year of the Black Fox. His ill omens seemed confirmed when the first baby born in the tribe that year was born mute. Still, he was an attractive infant. His mother named him Wind Dancer.

The harsh winter, which had mantled the plain with a
heavy blanket of snow, was still present the day Wind
Dancer was born. The parents of the mute child were disappointed with their son's affliction, but they loved him no less
than the parents of other newborns. Yet, as the time neared
to read his name along with the others before the tribal
bonfire, many families protested.

On a cloudy winter's day, and over the objections of
several tribal members, Wind Dancer's name was read before the assemblage. Thereafter, two incidents occurred. The
first was when the medicine man read Wind Dancer's name
aloud. At once, the overcast sky broke, allowing the sunlight
to appear. Although pleased, the people considered it a
coincidence, and after all, other names had been read as
well. The second thing which took place affected only the
shaman. Upon uttering Wind Dancer's name, the medicine
man believed the baby spoke to him. Momentarily stunned,
he nevertheless did not speak of it, but continued the ceremony, lest someone think he had become unbalanced.

After the festivities, the medicine man decided to tell the
chief his suspicions. With the chief waiting, the shaman
became embarrassed when he discovered that he couldn't
remember what he had heard. In fact, the harder he tried,
the less he was able to recall. As time passed, only a frag-
ment of the incident remained in his mind. The one detail he
could vividly recollect was feeling inwardly content and
happy the moment the infant spoke. He was convinced that
this was no ordinary child. When the winter at last released
its grip, and spring embraced the river valley, the medicine
man suspected that Wind Dancer was somehow responsible.
Happily, he changed his original ill omens on Wind Dancer
and predicted that the boy would someday bring honor to
his parents and his people.

The years passed, and Wind Dancer mastered his silent
affliction. He had become a handsome but somewhat mysterious young man. There were many stories about this boy
born mute in the year of the Black Fox. It was rumored that
although he could not speak, he could sing. Yet, those who
had heard his magical song were unable to recall what they
had heard. The only thing they could remember was that the
song had made them happy and content.

Among the other children born in the year of the Black Fox was a young girl called Bright Rain. She and other fifteen year old girls were being schooled by an old clan woman called a lodge mother. The lodge mother's task was to teach them the traditional responsibilities of Ndee women. This was necessary since it was nearing the time when a brave might propose marriage to them.

One day, the lodge mother was walking up a rocky hillside, showing the girls where and how to find certain plants. Accordingly, Bright Rain and a dozen other girls were attentively listening as the lodge mother explained the varieties of a particular herb. Suddenly, they were attacked by a timber wolf who bolted out from a nearby thicket. Knocking the lodge mother down, the wolf began chasing the screaming girls who scattered in terror. In their panic the girls plunged headlong down the hill. Fortunately, the tribe's young braves arrived at that very moment and saw that all but one girl had successfully eluded the wolf, who had finally caught and began mauling its victim.

For several seconds the braves froze in astonishment. One, however, acted instantly and decisively. It was Wind Dancer. Quickly seizing a sharp rock, he raced forward and flew onto the back of the wolf, pulling the beast and forcing it to release the struggling girl. The wolf instantly turned on him.

As the struggle raged and the combatants tumbled down the rocky slope, other braves joined their brother in the fight, which eventually ended with the death of the wolf. Afterwards, it was learned that several girls and braves had been injured. But the two most seriously hurt were Wind Dancer, who had engaged the wolf, and Bright Rain, its main victim. Despite his wounds, Wind Dancer rose unassisted from the foot of the hill and made his way back to its summit.

Reaching the top, Wind Dancer observed that a few of the camp people had arrived to help the injured. While they assisted the others, Wind Dancer slowly knelt over the tattered, seemingly lifeless body of Bright Rain. Gently he touched her bloodstained features wondering why he had never noticed her before. The girl remained unconscious, her breathing noticeably shallow. Yet despite her bruises, cuts, and gashes, the young woman radiated a quiet beauty which enchanted Wind Dancer. When the attendants reached Bright Rain, Wind Dancer stood to one side.

With some comforting words, the lodge mother, who had suffered a broken arm, was able to calm the crying girls. But when she looked on Bright Rain she paled and became visably alarmed.

"Do you think she is dead?" asked an attending tribal member.

"Who is she?" asked a second.

"Her name is Bright Rain," answered a girl bringing some herbs. "She is the youngest daughter of Gray Wolf, our chief."

"Ah, it is fitting then," remarked the tribal member, "to be killed by the namesake of your father. He will understand."

Angrily Wind Dancer knelt by the girl, making a sign language gesture which indicated that she would not die.

Silently, the lodge mother completed her assessment as others attended the boy. Counting the injured few already taken back to camp, she had not lost anyone, save perhaps Bright Rain. With noticeable distress, she looked upon the dying girl and began to weep. Unexpectedly, she also began a death chant. Those around her lowered their heads respectfully. Displeased with the premature decision, Wind Dancer stood up and soundly clapped his hands. The chant came to an abrupt halt.

Wind Dancer's sign language was well known and they easily understood that he requested silence. Furthermore, his gestures indicated the girl was not dead and that the Great Spirit would have to fight him for her life. He vowed he would always remain at her side.

"Do not make foolish promises, boy!" warned the lodge mother, annoyed at the brash young brave. "Has she opened her eyes since the attack? No! And judging from her wounds and deep sleep, she will soon be dead. Come, let her die in peace! Join us in her farewell song!"

"No!" was Wind Dancer's sign response. "I will not let her die!"

"Can you call her spirit back from the dead, boy!" the lodge mother challenged. "Are your powers strong enough to fight death itself?"

"If I must, I will!" the youth retorted in determined sign language. Kneeling again close to Bright Rain, Wind Dancer began to sing into her ear. Everyone leaned forward a bit to listen. However, Wind Dancer's song was barely audible and strain as they might, they heard little. To the lodge mother's experienced ear, the boy's song resembled a trilling more than a verbal chant. With his eyes tightly closed, the boy continued his strange melody, while the lodge mother observed what others were failing to notice: Wind Dancer had fallen in love with the wounded girl.

The lodge mother understood why Wind Dancer was trying to save the girl's life. His love was a powerful motive. Knowingly, she smiled, shook her head, and was curious to know what Wind Dancer was singing. Suddenly, to everyone's surprise, Bright Rain awoke. In obvious pain, she nonetheless recognized and stared up into Wind Dancer's eyes. Gratefully, she smiled, but said nothing. Custom forbade more. For Wind Dancer, it was enough. When the adults arrived, they all made the short trek back to the camp. Everyone began sharing stories and before long, the tale of the magical song was the talk of the camp. Despite inquiries, no one could be found who had actually heard it. Its discovery would have to wait.

The following day, Gray Wolf gathered the people together and while they sat listening, the old lodge mother related the incredible story. Praise was given to the valiant Bright Rain who had been mauled so severely. The braves who had assisted Wind Dancer emphasized their brother's strength and courage. Finally, when the story was exhausted, the chief asked to see the youth.

Bright Rain, who had recovered, was allowed to attend the gathering. Her mother placed her comfortably outside the tepee where she could observe the events. Her heart rate doubled as Wind Dancer, attired in his warrior's regalia, came to the fore of the great circle. The handsome lad was truly an unquestioned example of virile manhood. His fringed, decorative garments were intricately laced with blue, green, and red beads. His bone white chest plate was inlaid with wolves' teeth. His multi-colored headdress was impressively adorned. His face, streaked with white and black war paint, appeared menacing. The tribe's young women sighed as he passed and stood tall before the tribal chief.

"You, I am told," began the chief, "are the son of Dark Tree."

"I am called Wind Dancer, great chief," the boy announced proudly in sign language.

"Wind Dancer," whispered Bright Rain to herself.

"You have made your father proud, young man," proclaimed the chief, putting a hand on the boy's shoulder. "Your mother, Shadow on the Moon is also honored by her son's courage. This council seeks to reward your gallant deed. From this day, you are no longer a boy, but a man and a warrior."

The tribe exploded in thunderous praise, the echo carrying for miles in all directions. That day Wind Dancer took his place alongside the tribe's warriors, who cheered his inauguration. From her tepee, Bright Rain saw the tribe's adulation and was overwhelmed. She wept with inner joy, clasping her hands to her heart. Her mother knew she loved the silent warrior. That night a bonfire illuminated the camp for hours of celebration during which Wind Dancer's parents were repeatedly honored. This day would live in their hearts forever.

Throughout the following months Wind Dancer proved worthy of his position. Bright Rain's condition improved dramatically. Having her father's permission, Wind Dancer visited Bright Rain each day, and each day their love grew. As autumn approached, Wind Dancer assembled a great variety of gifts. With them, he stood ceremoniously before her father's tepee and openly proclaimed his desire to marry Bright Rain. The gifts being worthy, hearing no objections from anyone, and because his daughter was equally willing, the chief gladly accepted.

The young couple were soon married. But while the tribe celebrated the union, the curious playfully connived to overhear the mysterious song which Wind Dancer whispered daily to his bride. Everyone agreed there was magic in it, because each day Bright Rain grew ever more radiant. The medicine man believed the secret which inspired her happiness was the measure of the tribe's good fortune. Happily, the melody remained a mystery from all, except Bright Rain.

There was never a time when the married pair were not in love. When seen together, they always appeared joyful and loving. Their parents were pleased. When the brave was gone, his song kept his bride content until he returned. Moreover, when any child was sad, in pain or despair, Wind Dancer would sit, hover close to her or his ear and sing. Thereafter, the child's suffering disappeared, leaving the child overjoyed. However, when questioned, the child could not remember the song. Inner contentment was the child's lasting gift.

As the first snows of winter approached, Wind Dancer and his brother hunters saw to it that the tribe's reserves were well stocked for the lean months ahead. For many weeks, he and the others worked feverishly to supply the tribe with meat and staples. Their efforts were rewarded with grateful thanks from young and old. Now they could endure the winter's food shortages.

However, they had not foreseen life's disasters. News arrived that the chief's wife and several women had gone into the mountains to gather some rare winter herbs, but that they had become trapped in a narrow mountain gorge by an unexpected blizzard. Fearing they might die, the chief asked if anyone would hazard their rescue. To a man, all the braves volunteered.

Although many braves accepted the challenge of a winter blizzard, the chief selected only twenty. With abundant supplies, they trekked across the snow covered plain and started up the mountain. Stinging winds lashed at them relentlessly as they struggled upward. After three days they reached the snow line where the ascent became nearly impossible. With steadfast tenacity, the warriors followed their chief, determined to scale the towering obstacle.

Time after time they struggled forward a dozen yards or so only to have an unexpected avalanche drive them back. It became despairingly clear that the resolute group was gaining little ground, and time was becoming critical. The chief suggested they dismount and continue on foot. But this proved equally arduous. Each night several braves died in their sleep. Each day the hazardous ascent became costlier. As the dwindling few reached the summit, a horrendous snow slide claimed five more lives. The chief considered turning back, until he saw Wind Dancer forcing his ice covered body ahead like a spear point against the wall of unyielding snow. Carving a path through the waist-deep drifts, Wind Dancer brought the exhausted team to where the women were last reported. Frantically, everyone began searching the crevices, but it proved fruitless. The group was spent. Some decided the women were probably dead. Others thought they might have perished on the nearby cliffs. Studying the terrain, Wind Dancer suggested the women might have sought shelter in the caves.

Following Wind Dancer's hopeful suggestion, they discovered he was right, but to their dismay the women were found frozen stiff and near dead. The braves immediately lit several fires while Wind Dancer used his magical power. The chief prayed Wind Dancer's song was more than just rumor.

With the cave fires growing in strength, and having listened to the song of the Wind Dancer, the women awoke to realize they had been saved. But just as the warrior completed his song to the last woman, a terrific roaring shook the cave they were in. Turning instantly, the men saw a huge, monstrous grizzly bear entering the cave.

Without hesitating, all the warriors rushed the giant creature. Rising to its full height, the bear hurled the men back onto the walls with resounding thuds. Employing stone clubs, spears, and hand axes, three men bounded on top of the bear's massive shoulders and began hammering the brute. Momentarily confused, the grizzly countered angrily and without mercy, crushing one man's spine, while ripping another open with his teeth. The chief, the first to attack and be thrown back, awakened. He later recalled what happened next.

Disregarding his own safety, Wind Dancer hurled a spear deep into the huge beast's belly. The brave simultaneously leaped up, took hold of the bear's head, and thrust a flaming torch into its gaping jaw. The bear instantly recoiled in pain, shaking the other braves off and engulfing Wind Dancer in a smothering bear hug. The two combatants erupted from the cavern together and fell into the deep snow. Wind Dancer clung to the panic stricken bear while repeatedly driving his knife into its chest. The bear, howling in torment, continued to flay the warrior's body. Still Wind Dancer would not allow the animal to remove the smoldering torch. Turning one over the other, the unrelenting pair rolled down to the cliffs with the chief racing in pursuit. The remaining braves eventually caught up, only to watch in horror as the contenders, still locked in mortal combat, rolled off the cliffs and plunged to their deaths below.

For several moments the men stood in stunned disbelief. Then the chief began a death chant. The warriors added their voices and were unexpectedly joined by the recovered women who began to weep loudly. After several days, the stricken band left the mountain and crossed the broad plain in silence. No one said a word.

Two days later, the expedition arrived back in camp. The tribespeople were overjoyed that the chief had been successful in rescuing the women. But the wives of the warriors realized that of the original twenty warriors only four had returned. The tribe's older women comforted the younger ones and tried to explain the hazards the warriors had faced. The gathering broke into groups of wailing mourners who went off to begin funeral preparations.

When the bride of Wind Dancer arrived, she was greeted by the care-worn face of her father, who led a riderless horse. The chief and his wife were unable to say anything to their daughter. Bright Rain sadly realized that she would burn an empty funeral pyre. Holding back her tears and mounting sorrow, Bright Rain braced herself with courage and asked if her husband had died in battle.

The chief nodded. With a trembling voice, he explained that had it not been for Wind Dancer, the rest would not have returned. He had bravely sacrificed his life, so they might live. Had it not been for his enchanting song, the women would have died. Her father told her that the tribe would never forget Wind Dancer or his deeds. Bright Rain lifted her head and answered tearfully that she could not do otherwise.

During the next few days, funeral pyres were a constant reminder of the people's misery. The air was filled with collective wails and death chants. The whole tribe was burdened with unrelenting grief and it seemed as though it had lost its desire to live. The women were in perpetual sorrow, the children remained unhappy, and the men lacked ambition. The plain was devoid of life and the camp became a vale of lifeless forms. Bright Rain wore the face of utter despair. She did not smile and her people were dying of apathy. All this did not go unnoticed by the Great Spirit. He knew something had to be done.

Quite suddenly, the harsh winter inexplicably released its grip on the plains and yielded to a new spring. The land burst open with life and abundance. Trees blossomed early and flowers drew wide their floral patterns. The warmth of the sun and the resurgence of prairie grass meant the return of the buffalo. Soon, the "trembling earth" brought joy to everyone's heart. Life had returned, yet the tribe was puzzled. Why had the spring arrived earlier than usual?

The people wanted to learn the reason for this unusual phenomenon, but the medicine man and the tribal elders too were at a loss to explain it. Finally, the chief suggested they find and ask Bright Rain. Her sisters explained to everyone that she had begun taking long walks on the plains many days before. They did not know why, for she was very secretive about it, always insisting on going alone. They added that her visits to the meadows had preceded the sudden spring. Curious, the tribal women decided to search for her.

When at last the women discovered the whereabouts of Bright Rain, she was sitting contentedly amid a circle of spring flowers which carpeted the valley. As they drew near, they witnessed a miraculous sight. Bright Rain was resting quietly, staring far off into the distance when a tiny, almost imperceptible bird fluttered near her ear. The tiny creature's speed was astonishing. It darted with graceful ease forward and backward. From time to time it seemed to be poking its long thin beak into her ear as if whispering something to her. It amused Bright Rain so much, she burst out into joyful laughter.

The small bird had blue, green, and red body patterns. Its breast was white and it wore a crown of multi-colored feathers on its head. Its face was streaked with two black and white lines. In an instant, the women realized the small bird was wearing the same colorful costume that Wind

Dancer had used to declare his manhood. His departed spirit had indeed returned to his bride as he had promised. With his song, life had returned to her and to his people. The women promised to cherish this loving union forever.

My grandmother once said that in many of our Apache clan weddings of the past, it was customary for a husband to whisper a secret into his bride's ear which the two of them would share the rest of their lives. This unique tradition recalls the memory of a legendary bird whom the ancients called the Wind Dancer. We, of course, know it as the hummingbird.